Is Your Way In Your *Way?*

A Self Discovery Guide for Women on
How to Restore Yourself, Learn from Experience, and
Find Your True Self Again

By
Cassandra Crawley Mayo

Copyright © 2023 **Cassandra Crawley Mayo**

All rights reserved. No part of this publication may be reproduced, distributed, or transmitted in any form or by any means, including photocopying, recording, or other electronic or mechanical methods, without the prior written permission of the publisher, except in the case of brief quotations embodied in critical reviews and certain other noncommercial uses permitted by copyright law. For permission requests, write to the publisher, addressed "Attention: Book Rights and Permission," at the address below.

Published in the United States of America

ISBN 978-1-959173-15-1 (SC)
ISBN 978-1-959173-14-4 (Ebook)

Cassandra Crawley Mayo
222 West 6th Street
Suite 400, San Pedro, CA, 90731
www.stellarliterary.com

Ordering Information and Rights Permission:

Quantity sales. Special discounts might be available on quantity purchases by corporations, associations, and others. For details, contact the publisher at the address above.

For Book Rights Adaptation and other Rights Permission. Call us at toll-free 1-888-945-8513 or send us an email at admin@stellarliterary.com.

This book is dedicated to my parents, Herman G. Crawley and Kathryn "Kitty" Crawley, for validating the adage that the apple does not fall too far from the tree, regardless of the condition of the tree, whether tall, strong, weak, wide, deeply rooted, or uprooted. Thank you for being my trees.

ACKNOWLEDGEMENTS

Thank you to Dr. Myles Monroe for planting the seed about the graveyard being the richest place because there lie so many unfulfilled dreams. Writing this book was one of my dreams, so hearing this made me determined not to die with this dream unfulfilled; Bishop Joseph E. Grant for providing a Pentecostal platform that allows us to get out of our own way through the unadulterated Word of God; Willie Jolley for mesmerizing me with his eloquent public speaking and singing and inspiring in me a desire to be a transformational speaker and leader; Pastor John K. Jenkins Sr. for his character, integrity, and humility; my editor and writing doula, Ellena Balkcom, for being an enabler, stretching me out of my comfort zone to deliver more impactful and well-developed content;

Donald Ward for my ride or die through my Christian journey; Soror Adriane Brown, when I entered the real world you were there, and I thank God you still are present in my life; Soror Windy Deese, thank you for being my "keeping it real" buddy; Gwendolyn Davis, the older sister I never had; Kim Weaver, for critiquing my blogs in a constructive manner; Jacqui Williams, for holding me accountable; Kendyl Crawley Crawford, my millennial cousin, thank you for volunteering to read the manuscript draft. Your unapologetic feedback was succinct and to the point. You were the voice of a different generation, which is something we all need.

Last but not least Michael Mayo, my husband, for your patience with this endeavor. I continue to be in awe of how you manifested back in my life after years of fasting and praying for God to bless me with a lifetime partner. Only God knew you would be the one.

CONTENTS

PREFACE 1
INTRODUCTION: OUT-OF-BODY EXPERIENCE 4
Letter 1: DEAR WOMEN IN YOUR OWN WAY 12
Letter 2: DEAR YOUNG ADULT WOMEN 23
Letter 3: DEAR WOMEN WHO HAVE EXPERIENCED RACISM AND INEQUALITY 31
Letter 4: DEAR WOMEN WHO COMPARE YOURSELVES TO OTHERS 39
Letter 5: DEAR WOMEN WHO WEAR MASKS 46
Letter 6: DEAR WOMEN WITH ESTEEM BATTLES 51
Letter 7: DEAR WOMEN WHO QUESTION WHETHER THERE IS A GOD 58
Letter 8: DEAR WOMEN WHO CARRY OLD SCARS AND RESENTMENTS 67
Letter 9: DEAR WOMEN WITH PHYSICAL AND MENTAL HEALTH CHALLENGES 74
Letter 10: DEAR WOMEN WHO HAVE LOST A LOVED ONE 86
Letter 11: DEAR WOMEN WHO ARE CONFUSED ABOUT YOUR PURPOSE 94
Letter 12: DEAR WOMEN WHO ARE IN A GOOD PLACE 101
EPILOGUE 108
ENDNOTES 110

PREFACE

"For I know the plans I have for you, declares the Lord, plans to prosper you and not to harm you, plans to give you hope and a future" (Jer. 29:11 NIV)

May I ask you a question? If you were granted your heart's desires from this day forward, how would you like to be remembered by loved ones and those whose lives you may have touched? The depth of this question recently resonated with me, and I remembered reading a poem called, "The Dash," which I believe has touched millions of people's lives. Linda Ellis wrote this beautiful piece in 1996.

What inspired her to write what many call "uncomplicated poetry in a complicated world" was her revelation that too many people have a tendency to worry about making a *living,* rather than making a *life.* So, before you read any further, I encourage you to read her poem. Again, think about how you would like to live your *dash* for the remainder of your life.

THE DASH

Linda Ellis [1]

I read of a man who stood to speak at the funeral of a friend. He referred to the dates on the tombstone from the beginning ... to the end.

He noted that first came the date of birth and spoke of the following date with tears, but he said what mattered most of all was the dash between those years.

For that dash represents all the time they spent alive on earth and now only those who loved them know what that little line is worth.

For it matters not, how much we own, the cars ... the house ... the cash. What matters is how we live and love and how we spend our dash.

So think about this long and hard; are there things you'd like to change? For you never know how much time is left that still can be rearranged.

To be less quick to anger and show appreciation more and love the people in our lives like we've never loved before.

If we treat each other with respect and more often wear a smile ... remembering that this special dash might only last a little while.

So when your eulogy is being read, with your life's actions to rehash, would you be proud of the things they say about how you lived your dash?

I used to believe that the expression "Life is too short" was a cliché, until I experienced many dimensions of life. Specifically, when life started throwing curve balls that would catch me off guard, such as: witnessing the travesty of bad things happening to good people, racism, friend betrayal, coworker back stabs, jealousy, quandary of religious perspectives, death of a loved one, sickness and disease, health challenges, relationships gone bad, job loss, family drama, natural disasters, and so on.

One can get so caught up in the issues of life that you can lose focus on not only identifying the meaning of life, but your very purpose for being born. When this happens, we finally notice that time does not wait for anyone, and you may even feel yourself running out of time or near the end of your life's journey.

This is when 'Life is too short" becomes a reality. During this time in your life, I am hopeful you have discovered that trials and tribulations are inevitable, yet you still have choices of whether you will let *your way* get in your way or let unwise choices deter you from living your best life. We can be bitter or better. The choice is yours, but if better is your commitment, reflect on Jeremiah 29:11, and declare and decree what God has for you.

Another suggestion for really getting this lesson is to watch or rewatch the 1994 Stephen King movie, *The Shawshank Redemption*. There was a mantra that kept being repeated between the characters, Andy Dufresne, played by Tim Robbins, and Ellis Boyd "Red" Redding, played by Morgan Freeman, "Get busy living or get busy dying."[2] The scripture in Jeremiah and this mantra both reiterate intentionally living your life fully, knowing there is a divine plan.

There may be an opportunity or situation that compels or forces us to make a choice. You must believe the choice you make is for the better. In Proverbs 29:18 KJV[3], it states, *"Where there is no vision, the people perish."* That is a fact! Whatever our dreams and aspirations are will provide your life meaning, and when you are focused on that path regardless of all that is happening around you, you will give birth to something great.

I sincerely believe this can be the beginning of living your best life, free of self-imposed barriers. I tell you this because I know it to be true. It's nothing someone has told me, but what I have learned from experience. My vision was put in perspective by a quote from an unknown author found on a leadership poster, which reads, "Don't be afraid to start over. This time you are not starting from scratch, you're starting from experience."[4] The same is true for you, dear women who are ready to get out of your own way and get busy living.

INTRODUCTION: OUT-OF-BODY EXPERIENCE

The wicked flee when no man pursueth, but the righteous are bold as a lion.
(Prov. 28:1 KJV)

If being locked in a cage is equivalent to letting *your way* get in your way, I distinctly remember one day in an airport when I figuratively broke free and ran as if my very life depended on it. I never looked back to see if anyone or anything was chasing me. That is when I knew my life would never be the same again.

I knew it was time for latter rain and God's glorious purpose for me, as I recall making small talk with people on that day. I commented how the airport had become like my office, based on the amount of time spent there. That was a spot where I was able to get a lot of work done before arriving at my destination. My position at the time required a significant amount of travel over a nine- to ten-year span, approximately 75 percent of my time.

When you think of any of your travel experiences, specifically at an airport, on a train, bus, or cruise ship, have you categorized any of them as good, funny, bad, ugly, or perhaps even crazy? Regardless, there is usually a story to tell from these experiences. Despite how you would describe your experience, you have probably found the common denominator to be the people.

How often have you met someone during your travels and had an opportunity to get more acquainted with them? Like myself, perhaps your most enjoyable time during your trips have been with the people you have met. You may have even found, like me, that when you meet people, they end up telling you all their business. I have been spellbound by the transparency of people with me, a complete stranger.

During the sharing of their life stories, I recall a range of emotions from tears to laughter, anger, rage, and joy. I've always considered this an odd sort of gift. I can feel their emotions and can take them on internally, if I allow myself. If there is something, I can say to impart wisdom to make them feel better, I pounce on the opportunity to exercise that compassion for others.

In retrospect, you realize everybody has a story, even children. Although a stranger's transparency momentarily may place you in the position of therapist, you soon understand that they were open because they knew they would never see you again. Although many may have provided their contact information, hoping I would stay in touch. I often did not prefer to take their contact information. I usually did anyway, to not be rude. I knew in my heart of hearts that I did not have the time nor energy to stay in touch.

More importantly, I wondered if any of those conversations brought any solace because I considered some of my situations bad until hearing their stories. Who knows, maybe my approachable demeanor was subliminally intentional, in an effort to glean from their experiences. Sometimes it is simply good to know you are not alone in your life experiences. Whether you are validated in your tough situation or envious of someone else's, either way, the impact another person's story may have on your life can be powerful and insightful. Keep in mind, we all have a story, and one of mine was an encounter I once had at an airport. I would categorize this as the bad, and then it became ugly. Afterward, I broke out of my cage and started transforming into my freedom, as I pray you will be liberated to do in reading these pages.

On this particular day, I entered the old building of the Washington National Airport around 5:00 p.m. After a long week, I looked forward to going home to Chicago. I was never one to check my luggage with the airline, based on previous experiences of baggage not arriving at my destination. The first thing I would do is view my printed boarding pass for my flight number and check the departure board to determine the gate from which I would be departing. I then would go through security, allowing myself enough time in the event the lines are unusually long or passengers in front of me who are not familiar with the travel protocol are delaying the security line.

In other words, I knew the ropes and my limitations, so arriving late for a flight would not work well for me. Once I got through security this particular day, I rechecked the departure board to find my flight was going to be one hour and thirty minutes late. Leaving at that time would have me arriving in Chicago at 7:20 p.m. My other physical limitation was letting myself get too hungry. When this occurs, I not only have an internal break- down, but a bad attitude toward others.

Some of you may remember David Banner's character in the television adaptation of *The Hulk*. Banner was mild-mannered until someone provoked him to wrath. His famous line to warn his adversaries was, "You wouldn't like me when I'm angry!" Well, just call me Hulk when I'm hungry. You wouldn't like me, and neither do I like myself when I'm *hungry*. Needless to say, I decided to have dinner while waiting for my flight.

After eating, I was content and ready to get on the plane and go home. Once I arrived at my gate, I sensed something was wrong. I roamed the gate with my eyes and noticed some interesting facial expressions and body language. I looked at the board and saw "flight delayed." I looked outside to conclude that it was probably not the weather, and then double checked the weather on my blackberry to confirm that conditions in Chicago were stable as well. The travel agent informed passengers that the flight would only be one hour late.

Of course, several folks were upset by the fact that the flight was delayed, but there were also some frequent travelers who knew the drill. Approximately thirty minutes later, the agent announced that the flight was going to be delayed another forty minutes, due to weather conditions. I slowly sat up in my seat and thought that could not be true; after all, I had checked both departing and arriving city's weather conditions. I always thought if passengers were given accurate information, along with more specifics, that would be more helpful.

Clearly, the weather in Washington, DC and Chicago was fine. It would have been nice if they had offered a little more explanation of where the inclement weather was that was causing the flight to be delayed. When flight representatives share vague information, one can only assume they are not being truthful.

Then about thirty minutes later, there was another announcement: "The flight that was to arrive had mechanical difficulties." The agent spoke with confidence, though, that if they were unable to get the airplane repaired, they would replace it with another one. At that time, it was about 9:00 pm, and based on experience, ambiguity began to set in my mind about where this was going. The fact that I was getting tired did not help matters any, plus the airport was freezing. I was getting cold, and obviously the mice were, too, because they started coming out. For the record, I am afraid of mice; therefore, I knew this outcome was going to be pretty unforgettable, but I did not know yet how much so.

I observed my surroundings and noticed that folks were getting beyond frustrated. I also felt in my heart of hearts, like so many times during my travel experience, that the agents were not being upfront with the passengers, or they were being told what to say. I wasn't sure which. Regardless, this was a poor reflection on the airline. Then about thirty minutes later, the agents indicated that the flight was on its way and expected to arrive around 10:30-ish.

There was a sigh of relief, and I did another scan of the passengers again to observe that this was going to be a full flight. Around 10:00 pm, I was exhausted, and I realized that out of all my travel, I had never seen mice run around the airport like passengers. Witnessing this scene had me sitting in my seat with my legs, feet, luggage, and briefcase sharing a seat beside me. To say we were all tired and miserable would be an understatement.

Just as I started reflecting over my bizarre day and what frequent travelers go through, there was another announcement, *"Flight cancelled."* Oh my goodness, the reactions from passengers were bad. I sat there quietly to digest what happened and contemplating my next steps. The other frequent travelers and I appeared to not only know what to do, but most seemed to have the money to do what was necessary. However, so many other passengers did not have a clue.

Perhaps it would have been different if folks had lived in the Washington DC area and could go home, but the majority did not. It was obvious they had nowhere to go, had not eaten, and did not have a clue of what to do next. As exhausted as I was, I could have called my corporate travel agent to book a room for the night and flown out the next day. While assessing the agents along with the passengers, I guess it goes back to the most amazing parts of my travels being the people I met and how fascinating many were.

I was able to literally feel their emotions behind the stories they shared with me. I then realized they were experiencing another part to their story that I was indirectly a part of, and for some, it was getting to be ugly. There were others who appeared to be having some stress-related health issues, as evidenced by the protruding veins in their foreheads, red faces, and stress indicated through loud, angry outbursts. I continued to sit while the situation became even more chaotic, and I wondered if security or the police were going to show up at any moment.

What made matters worse, there were three agents, and in a nano second, we were down to two, as one had been preparing herself to leave due to her shift ending. Now there were two airline agents left to handle a full flight of people. Therefore, most of the passengers were at their mercy. I started feeling antsy, and I was not sure why.

Without thinking about it or even realizing it, I slowly got out of my seat and began walking over to the agent station in the midst of what appeared to be a warzone. This was my first out-of-body experience, but I clearly heard a voice inside of me question, "What are you doing?" The same voice responded, "I'm not sure." I then politely went over to one of the agents and asked her the following questions:

1. Did the airline have a contract with a nearby hotel(s), where the passengers could get a voucher and would not be responsible for expenses? If so, what were the names of the hotels, and what mode of transportation would they suggest?
2. Where would the passengers access the air- port shuttles?
3. What are the flights leaving the next day, what was the earliest flight, and was there a possibility that these folks would be able to get on that flight?
4. Were there complimentary travel vouchers that would allow the airline to possibly recover, since it did not appear that flight was cancelled due to weather?
5. Was there anything they can offer for those who had not been able to eat?
6. In the event folks had to pay for any of their expenses, what is the protocol for them to get reimbursed?
7. What are the phone numbers of the hotels? This was to make sure they had rooms available because it would have been terrible for folks to go to a hotel, and they did not have any vacant rooms.

Once I was able to get all of the facts, I got on the intercom, and made an announcement, providing them with information that would allow them to make a choice. Considering the options given, I asked them to form a line, based on their respective choice. There was pure silence, and I then helped the agents get organized and slowly tiptoed back to my seat and sat down.

For some reason, rather than going to a hotel, I was compelled to stay until all passengers were taken care of. Once that was done, the agent gave me a ticket for the first flight in the morning and thanked me for my help. That was around 2:00 a.m., and I was utterly exhausted. My adrenaline was so high, I did not realize what had happened until a passenger came over to me and said, "Ma'am, what you did was amazing."

To arrive at the airport the next morning to see many of the same folks I saw the night before, including a couple of the agents, was when the epiphany hit me. It was not so much the acknowledgment that I received when I arrived at my gate the next morning, but what stuck with me was an audible voice that kept repeating, *If you would only get out of your own way, you will witness the glorious plan and purpose for your life.*

Think about this, how often do you see or witness things, and you have the skill, knowledge, and competency to help when there is a need, yet you do nothing? No, my situation was not a life-or-death situation, but a high- stress situation that impacted lots of people. I am here to tell you that what I did, taking control of a problem and leading people to where they needed to go, was completely out of my comfort zone.

Furthermore, this was not my business. Now, please do not misunderstand me. If this had been in my work environment or a situation that I was personally or professionally responsible for, I would have risen to the occasion. However, one could not have paid or bribed me to do what I did that night *in an airport.* Contrarily, I may have stood there and complained, gotten agitated like so many others did, told my friends, and became boisterous, but not too bold in my actions. I am convinced that "hostile takeover" behavior I displayed was not of me.

I literally stepped aside and let God take over. If I had had a moment to think about it, I would have thought and talked my way out of it, letting *my way* get in the way. Like those self-imposed barriers that have so many of us stuck, I would have convinced myself to stay under the radar and maintain status quo. Realizing that the Spirit of God did this, I can only imagine what more He would do if I would allow Him.

The birth of *Is your way in your way?* originated at the airport on that day. This is the point where I decided to allow God to take over and asked Him to help me let go and let Him lead. I am now out of my cage, and I will not look back. I am running from how I used to be, and running toward how God wants me to be. I invite you on a journey to do the same, as you read through the pages to follow. Let the journey of self-discovery begin.

Letter 1:
DEAR WOMEN IN YOUR OWN WAY

(It All Begins with Your Backstory)

Train up a child in the way he should go, And when he is old he will not depart from it. (Prov. 22:6 NKJV)

I was raised in a small segregated suburban town by parents who did the best they could with what they knew. In other words, they were only able to parent with the awareness and understanding they had at that time. I preface by saying this because much of who we are today has to do with who our parents or the person/people who raised us were and how that impacted our childhood and backstory.

I can't emphasize enough how necessary it is to look back to better understand who you ultimately became. My parents were not perfect, because there are no perfect people. Nevertheless, parents play a significant role in our development, and again, most do the best they can. Growing up as an only child, the only wish I had was to have an older brother. I imagined him being my protector, having a lot of guy friends, and helping with the yard work, so I did not have to do it. My father was known for having one of the best-looking lawns in the community. My role was to sweep the sidewalks, and I always got blisters between my thumbs. My attention span was not so great. As opposed to sweeping in a timely manner, so I could be done, I spent more time looking at the people in their cars passing by the house.

There has been a lot of research on the pros and cons of having siblings versus being the only child. My perspective of many of their findings has been subjective in nature, but of course there will always be exceptions. Whether you were raised as an only child or with siblings, family dynamics, values, and our social economic environment are fundamental to how we view the world around us. Keep in mind that this developmental process is cyclical because your parents were once children too.

A Pew Research Center survey, conducted in 2014,[5] shows how the values of our parents are linked to their own ideological learnings. Regress a moment, and think about your grandparent's parents, and your great-grandparents' parents. Those ideological learnings go way back, and when you hear their stories, it may pique your curiosity. One family that comes to mind are the Kennedys.

The Kennedy family is known for their prominence in public service, business, and the political arena. They are also known for a lot of tragedy, but I do not consider that to be under the ideological effect, just unfortunate circumstances. When bad things consistently happen to families, folks categorize this as a "generational curse" or say it's the sins of the past catching up with them. If this is the case, who is to say we are not able to step out from the shadows of our past?

My point is you do not have to be bound by generational learning, curses, or past sins. You or someone you've spoken to may have even said, "This is just *my way*." But you can choose to not let *your way* get in your way. The self-imposed barriers preventing us from overcoming addictions, our past, molestation, abuse, infidelity, sickness, diseases, and so forth, do not have power over us. On the contrary, we have power over them, and we can make different choices than our parents and grandparents, yielding different outcomes for our lives. My personal experience from my childhood permeated throughout my adulthood, and you may find some similarities in your life.

Values spoken and demonstrated by my parents included: working hard, doing to others as you would have them do unto you, getting to work early in order to be on time, cleaning your room on weekends, expressing thanks when receiving gifts, and showing yourself friendly to have more friends. Some of their mantras were: association brings about assimilation, do not spend what you do not have, just because someone else has something does not mean you have to have it too, save your money, home should be maintained inside and out, meals are to be eaten together, and respect your elders.

Many of these may sound familiar to you. Also, attending church was not an option, regardless of what your activity may have been the night before Sunday morning. If someone in the family did not attend church services, we were visited by the pastor, my grandfather. My father was a preacher's kid, and an explanation had to be given if someone did not attend Sunday morning service.

Extracurricular activities were part of the fabric of my home life, such as ballet, tap, tennis, swimming, girl scouts, debutante, Jack and Jill, listening to jazz, and a strong suggestion to play the piano and violin. Although attempts were made regarding musical acumen, they were not successful. If you were raised in a two-parent household, you experienced different parental styles. Dad may have played the bad cop when you were told to ask his permission to do something your mom did not want you to do.

Mom was critical by nature, and I found myself wanting her approval so badly because the criticism was irritating and hurt at times. If you experienced that growing up, like me, you probably felt you were not able to do anything right. Have you ever found yourself walking on eggshells for fear of what might be said when you walked into the room? To avoid any confrontation, I was okay with her making decisions for me because voicing my opinion did not work well.

Dad was cordial and never showed emotions about much, so I found myself not showing much emotion either. He did not say a lot but was wise beyond his time. Opinions were not voiced, with the exception of my mom voicing hers to me and my dad, and physical affection was hardly ever shown. I always felt that giving me things was how they expressed their love, such as providing material things and presents for holidays and birthdays. Despite the criticism, I considered my mom and I close, like partners in crime. We did a lot of things together, and one of the most memorable was shopping. We would shop until we dropped, and there were times that shopping bags had to be hidden from my dad.

Although Mother was the matriarch of the family and the glue that made sure both sides of the family stayed connected, her heart of gold caused her to give the shirt off her back. And I recall my dad being frustrated with her spending habits. I surmised this was why shopping bags had to be hidden. My dad was big on saving, investing, and handling his business. Still, after dinner, I would try on my new clothes and model in front of my mom, and sometimes I would even go to the family room and model for my dad. While watching, his only show of emotion would be a slight smile. In response to my question of how I looked, he would simply nod and say I looked nice.

I mention my childhood because it is so critical to understanding the choices I later made, the way I perceived life and relationships, and the woman I ultimately became. Have you ever engaged in an exercise where you were asked to describe your backstory in your adult years? This reveals a narrative history of how you became who you are and why you act and think as you do. Like in a movie, this is the part of your story that led to the plot and climax of your journey. Although an astounding exercise, this does not mean you will always be satisfied with every element of your journey. However, understanding why you are the way you are may help everything make a lot more sense.

Needless to say, there may be aspects of your behavior and character traits you would like to adjust; yet it may be difficult because it has become *your way*. These behaviors may affect or impact the way you live or your relationships, as it did in my life.

You may find it difficult, but it is not impossible. You may see some behaviors in yourself that you wish were different.

This may be a time to adjust how you use your authentic voice, show up in your life as God would have you do, be more assertive, and not be concerned with what other people may think or say about you. When you were in your late teens, weren't you looking forward to becoming self-sufficient and independent? Like many, I felt attending college would be my ticket to independence. In preparation for college, I wanted to go to a historically black college or university (HBCU). This was driven by the fact that when I attended South Morrison Elementary School, I was the only black kid.

When this happened to me, I was overwhelmed at the idea, yet my saving grace was that my mom was employed there as the only black teacher. Have you attended a school or been in an environment where you were the minority? I took comfort in knowing my mom would have my back; therefore, I felt no harm would come to me. Although I was young, I knew I was subject to racism, particularly because sending my mom off to an all-white school was part of an experiment with integrating schools. How often were you told you had to do something as a child, and you knew you had no power to tell your parents *no?*

I was not asked, nor did I want to be a part of this experiment; I was recruited. My mother was not comfortable with me being home alone after school, feeling that adult supervision would be needed, considering the distance of our home from South Morrison. In a hindsight view of this reason, I will say, *Mom knows best.* Based on my experience in an all-white school, I was itching to find out what it would be like to attend an all-black school. I later applied, got accepted into and attended an HBCU.

COLLEGE DAYS

When you graduate from high school, you may not have any idea what is next for you. What I knew for sure was I was going to college, yet I did not have a clue what vocational path I wanted to pursue. We all recall being younger and being asked what you want to be when you grow up. Perhaps you even felt obligated to know, so you would offer up something. When reality set in and you were given an opportunity to prepare yourself for the real world, you remained clueless.

Clueless is where I found myself, so I decided to major in business administration because of the flexibility and versatility it offered. Due to the adaptability of that major, I knew I would eventually find something. In the meantime, I focused on my academics and enjoying the college life. I loved being a part of an HBCU environment, particularly because I did not have a point of reference for being in a majority population environment.

The comradery and similar backgrounds and cultures were refreshing. It was a natural fit, and many lessons were learned about not having any expectations. When you don't have a lot of personal experience within an environment, or in a situation, you go in wearing a clear set of lenses. In other words, when you do not have any preconceived notions, it allows you to learn and grow from differences. From that point, you form your own inferences and opinions. This also creates a space for self-development, progression, evolution, and propagation.

During my sophomore year, I pledged AKA (Alpha Kappa Alpha Sorority, Inc.). My pledging period was nine weeks, and that did not include the "rush" process that may last from three days to two weeks, where sororities or fraternities recruit potential members. To say the least, pursuing membership was intensive, and the communal aspect of pledging with thirty-two young women on my line was a major adjustment. Nevertheless, there were pros and cons.

Skills that I attained transferred into the real world, such as networking, collaboration, and teamwork, relationship building, and the ability to balance academics with social activities. Memories of my college days are priceless, and the AKA sisterhood continues to exist. You too may have found being a part of a sorority, group, or organization rewarding and impactful and an affiliation that offered you a sense of accomplishment.

Upon entering my last year of undergrad, I thought there would be some type of revelation of what I wanted to do, but there was none. I enjoyed learning, but I remained clueless as to what I wanted to do—but God. I took advantage of all the resources college had to offer, such as the career development office and internship programs. While in school, I did take advantage of an internship program where I worked a semester and attended school the next semester. When the program was over, I was offered a job when I graduated. Have you experienced being offered an opportunity, and your heart said no, but your head said yes? You may have had a similar situation, where there was a conflict in your psyche.

This time, I went with my heart, and turned the internship position down. The faculty was so supportive of me and encouraged me to keep applying with companies that were recruiting in the career development office. There was one advisor who offered some insight that impacted me for years to come. I was told, "You may be offered a job opportunity because of how you look, not how smart you are." Even if the reverse was said, their intentions don't matter as much as how you receive or interpret what's being said.

This is when my work ethic went overboard because I was trying to prove how smart I was. Regardless, I continued to apply for job opportunities that appeared to be a good fit. My plan to address not knowing what I really wanted besides being happy was to literally just *go with the flow,* and *let the chips fall where they may.* In hindsight, my indecisiveness impacted many aspects of my adult life. I will share the benefits and hindrances indecisive ness had on my life in upcoming letters. There was one thing I was certain of, and it is that I would venture out and live on my own after graduating. My determination paid off, and I was offered a job. I landed a job with one of the "Big Three" automobile manufactures prior to graduating.

However, a prerequisite for that position was to relocate to Birmingham, Alabama.

KEY MESSAGE: Your Back story is Critical

Understanding the critical backstory of why you are the way you are will offer insight into who you have become. No, we cannot choose our childhood or the circumstances that make up our early experiences and memories. Yet, these collective events and impressions form the core and foundation of the way we think, decisions we make, the relationships we form and the type of parents we ultimately come to be.

Let me be clear. In the event you believe your past is preventing you from living a joyous, fulfilled, and meaningful life, that is simply not true. You absolutely have the power to step out from the shadows of your past. Not only can you step out, but you can step into a glorious future free of *your own way*.

The same is true of your parenting skills. You are not bound by the way you were raised. If there are certain values and characteristics you would like your children to have, be conscious about emulating them. Remember, they will remember and be more impacted by what you *do* than what you *say*.

The Word of God reminds us that when you bring up a child in the way they should go, they will not depart from it when they are older. You may not see the evidence now, but you will sooner or later, so cut yourself some slack and forgive yourself of any mistakes We all make them, and there is no map or blueprint to parenting. In fact, you may even notice yourself turning into your parent/guardian in some respects, even imitating those things that once irked you growing up. Or maybe you consciously do the opposite of what your parents did.

- Reevaluating your backstory is a powerful and critical way to better understand the woman you

are today and to change *your way* where necessary.
- It is not about where you start, but where and how you finish. Your childhood, past or backstory does not define you or your future.
- Know that you will not be perfect as a parent, but give yourself and your children grace, knowing you are helping shape your child's backstory.
- Love intentionally by backing up what you say with action.

Regardless of your backstory, it is important to know today that love is an action, so in all your personal relationships, say it often, but show it even more.

SCRIPTURE TO LIVE BY:

Proverbs 22:6 (NKJV)
Ephesians 6:4 (NKJV)

The Word of God says, "Train up a child in a way that he should go, and when he is old he will not depart from it." (Prov. 22:6 NKJV). This simply means that if you raise a child according to the Word of God and in the admonition and reverence of our Lord and Savior, he will always return to God, regardless of the path he takes. Another well-known scripture reads, "And you, fathers, do not provoke your children to wrath, but bring them up in the training and admonition of the Lord." (Ephesians 6:4 NKJV).

The Amplified version translates this to mean that parents should not exasperate children to the point of resentment with demands that are trivial, unreasonable, humiliating, or abusive. It goes on to say show no favoritism or indifference but bring them up tenderly with loving kindness in the instruction and discipline of the Lord. I said in the key message that there was no map or guide to parenting, but it looks like we have one here.

KEY MESSAGE: Association Brings About Assimilation

Proverbs 13:20 conveys how association brings about assimilation. I have learned that the power of association is real and critical. Never underestimate the impact you may have in any environment or organization. The cycles of life and various circumstances may cause you to say about yourself or others to say about you, "I knew you when ...." There could be a time in your life where the person you "knew when" becomes famous or successful. This association can then be a cause for exhilaration, hope, empowerment, nostalgia, or a credible experience in a time in your life when needed most.

Their gain can make you proud, lift you up, and you may even become a part of it somehow. This is what I know:

- The right or wrong associations can cause a shift in perspective and mind-set for the better or worse.
- Assimilating does not mean you become a sheep. On the contrary, your ability to lead and think independent of the association will get keener over time.
- What we don't want to do is play the comparison game. It only leaves you feeling stagnant and stuck in your own way.
- Invest in your communications and social skills because it has the propensity to yield opportunities and benefits
- As we know, there are benefits to financial investing. There are also benefits for investing and building meaningful relationships.
- Do not burn bridges because you may need to cross them again.

Because we never know when an association might serve to benefit us or we might be used in a season to benefit others, treating people well at every stage and station of life is essential to getting out of and staying out of your own way.

SCRIPTURE TO LIVE BY: [6]

Proverbs 13:20 (NKJV)
Proverbs 27:17 (NKJV)

The Word of God says, "He who walks with wise men shall be wise, but the companion of fools will be destroyed" (Prov. 13:20 NKJV). This simply means that you will *become* the company you keep. Another well-known scripture reads, "As iron sharpens iron, so a man sharpens the countenance of his friend" (Prov. 27:17 NKJV). The Amplified version translates this to mean that one man "influences" another through discussion. None of us were put here to be an island, and these scriptures remind us of how interdependent and interconnected we are and should be to one another, when we are of sound mind and good, Godly judgment.

Letter 2:
DEAR YOUNG ADULT WOMEN

(Welcome to the Real World)

"Be strong and of good courage, do not fear nor be afraid of them, for the Lord your God, He is the One who goes with you. He will not leave you, nor forsake you" (Deut. 31:6 NKJV).

When I entered the real world, I learned the Word of God does not go void. We all have a story, and mine encompasses the bad, the good, and the ugly. I chose to use this book to not only share mine, but to be of service as an agent to empower you to live the life you were created for.

When my airplane landed in the 1970s at what was then called the Birmingham-International Airport in Birmingham, Alabama, my entrance into the real world began. In other words, I was no longer living under the shadow of parents or guardianship, yet unbeknownst to me, whether subconsciously or consciously, I was now living under the shadow of almighty God.

If you come from a family of strong believers of God, and you have heard a loved one say, "I have given you over to the Lord," then you understand what I mean by living under the shadow of God. *Again, welcome to the real world, young adult.* When I walked off the plane, I was a bit skittish for three reasons, and you may find some similarities while entering your independent or transitional stages of life.

Number one, moving away from home to a faraway place is not as simple as driving two to three hours to visit the familiar.

Second, not knowing anyone and having no friends or relatives adds another level of complexity. And finally, knowing the history of "strict enforcement of total segregations" in an area or environment you have decided to call home, can be scary when it is unclear how your life may be impacted.

Making the decision to move to Birmingham, Alabama, was my choice, despite civil rights images that ruminated in my heart and mind, such as protests and the 16th Street Baptist Church bombing, where four little black girls were killed. In addition, police rampantly beat black people, dog attacks, and fire hoses were used on peaceful demonstrators for the sole purpose of control and suppression of those fighting for the basic human rights of justice and freedom. Regardless of the choices we make, life goes on, and we move forward to live life the best we know how.

The word *sacrifice* becomes a reality and living within your means is absolutely necessary when relocating and sustaining a lifestyle independently. A great example is finding yourself a place to live. Has there been a time when someone recommended a place for you to live, and you thought, *I would not recommend this place to anyone I knew.* I recall a blatantly racist experience I had during my search to find a place. When I completed my rental applications in a certain area of town, I was told there were no vacancies, although I could afford it. I shared my dilemma with my manager and told him a specific place I liked and how it was also convenient to the job.

A day later, I received a call from the property manager of the complex informing me that an apartment had just come available. I was so excited, but my excitement quickly deflated when I found out they had a new development within the complex that had an enormous number of vacancies. Could that have been a situation of, *it is not what you know, but who you know?* This was certainly true in my case. After moving in, I discovered it was being redlined, meaning they restricted their housing availability to tenants they did not deem as a financial risk. This meant African Americans were being denied access.

I realized that if I wanted to be successful with my fundamental desires, major adjustments to my personality had to be made. The desires of my heart would not come easy being an introvert, particularly not knowing anyone. Extrovert or introvert, one tends to rise to the occasion if your life depends on it. Ladies, finding a hair salon and shopping was not only therapeutic, but necessary.

I was certainly out of my comfort zone being an introvert in a new city where I did not know anyone. When out and about, a line I would use was, "I'm new to the area. Do you have any recommendations for a salon, boutique, church or medical doctor?" How many times have you crossed someone's path, and admired something about them, such as their hair, clothes or energy? A compliment was always a great segue to gain needed information.

Like my mom used to say, "If you want friends, you have to show yourself friendly." These small steps may transform you into an outgoing person, even if you are still introverted at heart. You may find yourself meeting so many people that you start introducing people to others. As a result of a personality I did not know was in me, I became known as the girl about town who knew everyone. Ironically, I started dating someone who was well known as well. Recall times in your life when you would say to yourself, *life is good.* And wham, before you know it, life happens, and it is not so good anymore.

Working in a capacity you enjoy, performing well, and progressing to be promoted can be coined as the eye of the storm until the unexpected occurs, and the storm rages and causes devastation. Imagine receiving the news that the organization you are working for is undergoing downsizing because of an economic downturn, and you land in that number of layoffs. It is like a rug being pulled from underneath you, yet you still have the audacity to exude a sense of entitlement.

You question how they can do this to you, and you may even dare them in your mind. This is exactly what happened to me. Not only did I have a sense of entitlement, but also distorted thinking in regard to being stranded deep down in the South, miles away from home. I was thinking I should have accepted the internship offered and by now I should have an idea of what I want to pursue next. But, I didn't.

Since my experience had been in a management trainee program, I surmised that following this route was probably a good idea. Glory be to God, another opportunity was granted quickly, which was branch manager trainee at the largest bank in the state of Alabama. Finding yourself working in another position you enjoy immensely and literally seeing the succession taking you to levels you could not imagine is such an exhilarating, magical feeling.

The magic dissipated quickly when I was called to the human resources office at our corporate headquarters. I was anticipating a transition to my own branch, only to find out I had to be released—again. Imagine working for two different organizations and being released from both. I was downsized from one, and the other was not able to secure bonding on my behalf. I was arrested in college for stealing a shirt, and that disqualified me from working at the bank. If you've ever been released from a job, your reason for being released may be different than my reasons, but nevertheless just as emotionally devastating.

Not only did my past catch up with me, but what I had done scared me so badly that I vowed to never steal another thing in my life. I did not know whether I would be able to get another job or how to overcome what I had experienced. At that time, I felt stuck and in my own way mentally, because of shame and confusion. I was in disbelief that after all the studying, preparation, and smooth jumpstart to a bright future, I still found myself here—scared and jobless. I prayed a lot and got closer to God during the entire ordeal. I was so ashamed to tell anyone what had happened and why I was unemployed.

Looking back, I strongly believe that if I had confessed earlier, I may have gotten another job sooner than I did. Nevertheless, I still had to pay for my transgressions years later, and it was humiliating.

We all make mistakes, and there are times when we judge others that have made them as well. If you are reading this letter, you too have made them, and some mistakes continue to be a secret thorn in your side, and others you were courageous enough to tell someone. It's time to get out of your own way. Talking about it with someone is helpful and has powerful benefits. Thank God you have overcome some mistakes and poor choices, and God's grace and mercy saw you through, just like He saw me through.

It took me nine months to find another job, and although it happened long ago, I remember it like it was yesterday. Fast forward, I ended up working in different capacities in corporate America over thirty-plus years. One goal I set for myself was to retire at the age of fifty-five, and my mission was accomplished. In retrospect, I ask myself *How in the heck did I make it this far*? What I know for sure is, it was by the grace and mercy of God, who enabled me to be adaptable and come out of my comfort zone during some adverse situations. I now understand that this is how the Father assists us in getting out of our own way during pivotal times of our journey.

During my years of work experience, I attained a Master of Science degree in Organizational Development, a graduate certificate as a Johns Hopkins Fellow in Change Management and a Certificate in entrepreneurship. Throughout my career, I immersed myself in taking career development classes and became active in several professional affiliations. By no means am I underestimating the power of education because without it, I would not have accomplished what I have today. Looking back, I enjoyed learning despite the challenges that came with it. I felt like a kid in a candy store when I started pursuing advanced degrees.

It was exciting, exhilarating, motivating, and such an empowering experience for me. For me seeking advanced degrees many years after I had received my under- graduate degree enabled me to have a better sense of appreciation. It aided me to apply my learnings, and I grew so much from it.

I'm certain having had years of work experience prior to going back to school brought more richness to the experience. I also noticed after I would get a degree or a graduate certificate, it catapulted me to a new level spiritually, emotionally, and mentally. What an accomplishment and sense of empowerment I felt when I was done with a class or training. I became so much more confident in my abilities.

During my more than two decades working in "Corporate America," I held various positions of increasing leadership and responsibility. These various positions opened opportunities for me to reside in the following cities: Washington, DC; Birmingham, Alabama; St. Louis, Missouri; Newark, Delaware; Norfolk, Virginia.; Fairfax, Virginia; Hunt Valley, Maryland; Gaithersburg, Maryland.; Chicago, Illinois; and Laurel, Maryland.

One would think I was in the military, but I was in the army of the Lord. I will explain that further in my other letters to you. It was imperative for me to share how my professional history was packaged so that the trajectory of events that will be shared will provide you with some perspective. I realize now that I identified myself with what I *did,* although that was not who I *was.*

For my entire career, working eight hours per day became unheard of, and eleven-plus hours a day became the norm. I was like a hamster that was conditioned to the pace, and it was literally difficult to stop. My hamster syndrome attributes were as follows: disciplined, focused, committed, loyal, results-oriented, strong work ethic, and a workaholic.

I started realizing that pace was not working for me in certain junctures of my career. I started questioning whether it was time for me to do something different. I no longer had peace in my situation, and for those who have not had peace of mind, you know how unsettling this is.

To work in a capacity where my heart was no longer there, I thought it was not only unfair to me but also to the organization. I felt so torn knowing that there was something else out there but not knowing what exactly. Being a type A personality and unable to figure out specifically what that should be, I was hurt and frustrated. Even though I have never birthed a child, I felt that I was in labor.

The water had broken, but I was still waiting for the baby to be delivered. So, for the woman who has birthed a child, I'm certain you can feel my pain. In the midst of the pain, I started experiencing health issues and was diagnosed with something that only time would tell the outcome. I cried out to God multiple times and was not able to shake what continued to resonate in my spirit. *If you would just get out of your own way and let Me take over.*

Beyond this letter, ladies, it is critical for me to not let *my way* get in my way. What you are about to read are certainly things that I would not disclose to anyone except my closest friends, and they do not even know all of the stories. I'm led to believe that what's going to be exposed is necessary. Knowing that the stories, which are mine, will be similar to yours, and knowing undoubtedly that God's Word does not go void, I was confused as to why my favorite scripture, John 10:10, was not manifesting at this point in my life.

The scripture reminds us that although the thief comes only to steal, kill, and destroy, the Son came that we might have and enjoy life more abundantly. There had to be a reason why I wasn't experiencing life more abundantly. I was miserable, and even though this was not the only time that I would be at my wits end, I knew this time if I was going to live out my latter days in an abundant manner, I'd need to ask God to help me. This cry was really from my heart and not my head, and so my bootcamp of faith, submission, and obedience began. So, writing this book is another step of obedience to God.

KEY MESSAGE: Be Mature and Developed, Not Deficient

In order to mature and develop, without deficiency and as whole as possible, we will have to go through some things. It's a plight none of us can avoid, yet God in His omniscience, has made provision for us during these trials and tribulations. Not only have we been given the Lord Jesus Christ, but we have the Holy Spirit to comfort and guide us through times of pain or doubt. God even took it a step further by giving us one another as godly counsel to lean and depend on, and ultimately help each other grow through our trying times. This is what I know.

- What's done in the dark comes to the light eventually.
- Be courageous enough to talk about what you are going through with someone. It could be helpful and yield powerful benefits to them and you.
- God's grace and mercy will see you through.
- Do not judge others when they are being challenged so that you won't be judged during your difficult times.

When all is said and done, we are our brothers' and sisters' keepers. Let's take good care of one another, demonstrating the love of Christ.

SCRIPTURE TO LIVE BY:

James 1:1–4 (MSG)

In the book of James 1:1–4, the Message translation states, "Consider it a sheer gift, friends, when tests and challenges come at you from all sides." You know that under pressure, your faith-life is forced into the open and shows its true colors. So, don't try to get out of anything prematurely. Let it do its work so you become mature and well developed, not deficient in any way.

Letter 3:
DEAR WOMEN WHO HAVE EXPERIENCED RACISM AND INEQUALITY

"If someone says, 'I love God,' and hates his brother, he is a liar; for he who does not love his brother whom he has seen, how can he love God whom he has not seen?" (1 John 4:20 NKJV)

When entering a new juncture or significant life event, like a new job or career, new surroundings, moving to a new town or area, trepidation becomes a partner in the process. Change is a part of life, whether we want it or not, yet when we embark on the unfamiliar, those natural instinctive feelings are to be expected. Needless to say, you decided to take on what you believe is a great opportunity and to courageously take the world by storm. Although we live in a "hurry up society," there will be situations in our lives that ring true.

The words of Phil McGraw "Life is a marathon, not a sprint." [7] In the midst of life's adventures, there are usually what I would like to coin as "life interruptions," such as experiencing racism and inequality. Throughout my career, I relocated seven times, and everywhere I resided, inequality followed, and it still does. It was hard to believe I was experiencing racism over and over again, now without the protection of my mom like I did when I was the only black kid in my elementary school. I will share some of my experiences that may sound familiar if you have endured anything similar. If so, think about how you felt, as well as how you chose to react during those oppressive times.

Experience 1

When I was officially hired to be the general manager for Marriott Courtyard Hotels, I was so excited. Being a hotel manager would have sufficed for me, but when I was offered the general manager job I was blown away. Although I had management experience, the thought of overseeing a hotel was daunting for me. Nevertheless, when I was offered the job by the hiring manager, my response was "Yes, what's next," and his response, "Great, I met my quota." I was perplexed by his reaction, yet I did not give it a second thought. My endeavor was to learn the business and do a great job. By God's grace, I did a wonderful job and was recognized for my performance numerous times.

Eventually, I was transferred to the flagship Courtyard Hotel, which was close to Marriott Headquarters. I was so focused on dotting all of the I's, crossing all of the T's and managing the hotel like I was the owner. The thought that my employment could have been meeting a diversity quota was the farthest thing from my mind. In retrospect, I was in a bubble, performing in a capacity that exceeded expectations.

I believe nothing happens before it's time because before I knew it, I was the first African American female to run a Marriott Courtyard hotel. My accomplishments changed the lenses for many I came in contact with, regardless of race or color. Although I was naïve, I still am so glad that I did not get hung up on the statement made by the human resources manager, "I met my quota." Regardless, I was given an opportunity, and it opened doors for many others who looked like me. I feel blessed to have paved the trail.

Experience 2

I was promoted to a management job, and I relocated again to a place where I knew no one. In order for the company to save money, as opposed to placing me in a hotel as a single occupant, I moved into a hotel room with my boss, an Asian woman, until I found a place to live. When I arrived, I was shown where I would be sleeping to discover I was being placed in a walk-in closet. There was plenty of room to sleep in the bedroom area and being placed in a closet made me feel like a castaway. I was confident they would have never offered this option to my boss or a white woman. Today, I probably would have protested more vocally, but I don't regret my response, as my boss ended up genuinely liking and respecting me, forming a valuable relationship later.

Experience 3

When a guest in the hotel I managed was over-the-top upset about an issue within the hotel, there were a couple of options made available to get what they felt would be an appropriate resolution. Number one, write a letter to Mr. Marriott, or number two, see the general manager. There were several times while walking toward them to address their concern, I could see that their expressions were like deer in the headlights. There was one guest (white female) who looked at me before I was even able to ask how I may help her and said,

"No wonder the hotel is not being run correctly," and she then walked away. And we all know she didn't make this snap judgement based on anything except the color of my skin. I actually laughed to myself, thinking *here we go again,* which proves that what doesn't kill you, only makes you stronger.

Experience 4

By mistake, I was given a document that listed all salaries of general managers, only to find I was paid the lowest in spite of my tenure and performance. I felt comfortable approaching the chief financial officer in the company with this information and eventually received a sizable amount of retroactive pay for the salary discrepancy.

Experience 5

I was being trained for a management position by other managers in an organization, and it was implied by one of them, a white guy, that if I ever was to be promoted to upper management, the responsibilities would be too hard for me as a woman. Once I was promoted, he ended up reporting to me, and thirty days later, he resigned from his position.

Experience 6

Working in the position of vice president, client relations, one of my responsibilities was to meet with the senior executives of a hospital system. When I introduced myself as working out of the office of the president for my company, the chief executive officer asked me whether I was my boss's administrative assistant. When I responded that I wasn't, he immediately turned red, indicating his embarrassment.

Experience 7

I had been promoted to another position, and the vice president of the division was told by my colleagues (white men) that I was not a good fit for the job. They shared that I was an embarrassment to the organization. The vice president then met with me and suggested I go back to the industry I had previously worked in. Being humiliated about that news, I cried and asked if it would be okay to go home early and get back with him in the morning about his request. I decided to stay, and it turned out that the vice president would always summon me if there was a problem with a client, because he was confident I would resolve it.

Experience 8

Being a proud new owner of a car, the registration process included having car insurance. With my good driving record, Allstate would not insure me, and they would not provide an answer as to why. Until this day, Allstate will never be my insurance company of choice for this reason.

Have you ever thought that if racism and inequality did not exist, how far we would we be as a nation, despite our history of legalized slavery? There continues to be disparity regarding how far our country has come on racial equality. Unlike white Democrats and Independents, white Republicans believe there have been enough changes made toward racial equality (Pew 2016). Blacks, on the other hand, are skeptical as to whether there will ever be true racial equality in this country, which is why the *Black Lives Matter* movement continues.

Not having walked in the shoes of the oppressed, many are oblivious to the impact of racial injustice. The reason many perspectives are different is because those who are not of color have not experienced injustice because of their race. However, other groups have also been treated inhumanely and callously by others, such as the physically disabled, mentally ill, alcoholics, drug addicts, and homosexuals. It's unfathomable that certain societal groups believe it is okay to pay women, Blacks, or any of these other groups mentioned less for performing the same job.

If you know of someone or have experienced being treated in an inhumane way, how did it make you feel? Would you consider that as being treated unfairly because of what your lot or fate in life may be? Being subject to moral, ethical, and illegal exclusion has consequences emotionally, physically, and spiritually. Think about the images of racism, in addition to inhumane actions of certain groups toward others. How often do you wonder where the hate and prejudices come from, or better yet, why people are like that, particularly when you know people are not born with it?

We eventually see it is learned behavior. How dare someone make quick judgement of the characteristics of an entire race or group and label them as inferior or superior. Not being extended basic human rights is painful enough, and then add on top of that discrimination based sheerly on what society deems as different or abnormal, which is not what God would call it. Personally, this is hard for me and many others to wrap our heads around, when what we all really want is so basic—equality. In the famous words of Martin Luther King, Jr., "I look to a day when people will not be judged by the color of their skin, but by the content of their character." [8]

The experiences cited as my examples were just a few of many. Imagine being judged by the color of your skin, ethnicity, and not your character as a way of life. This would mean always having to prove you have what it takes to perform effectively in the role you have been assigned. How exhausting when you know you are treated unjustly, yet you are still expected to perform with a good attitude, despite being the minority and unable to use your voice for fear of losing your job. When your performance is stellar and your outcomes contribute to the bottom line, it makes you wonder what it takes to get respect for something you are gifted to do.

KEY MESSAGE: Try Something Different

When you are constantly watching your back for fear of what someone else is thinking, it stifles progress and creativity. You must then get out of your head and your own way and try something different. When you have no one to talk to about how you are feeling, many may find comfort in the Word of God. It is made clear that all of us were made in the image of God (Gen. 1:27), and that He is no respecter of persons (Acts 10:34). This is what I know.

- Get in the Word of God, and gain confidence in who you are in Him and as His creation.
- Find an affinity or diversity resource group to share your experience and draw from the knowledge and resources of others who understand.
- Embrace diversity and inclusion training. Go in with an open mind.

- Seek counsel on the best way to handle unfairness effectively before reacting.
- Maintain your control when facing bias and injustice, through prayer, self-talk, and walking away if necessary if you believe the situation will get worse.
- Build and develop effective relationships in your work- place and organizations you are part of. You may find one to be an influencer, decision maker, sponsor, and or an ally in a life situation you encounter.
- Keep in mind the saying: do not burn your bridges, because you may need to cross them again.
- Do not underestimate the power of relationships.
- Follow the Golden Rule: do unto others as you would have them do unto you.
- Be the change you want to see in the world; be an activist and community servant.
- Know it is ok to have tough conversations about racism and inequality.

When you are silent, it may convey you are ok with the situation and or circumstances. Or you are ok with the status quo remaining.

The *Say Their Names* racial injustice memorial campaign and the litany of victims killed by police brutality or by non-po lice, such as Travon Martin, Ahmaud Arbery, and Breonna Taylor, continues to be a pandemic within a pandemic. As a result, actionable awareness has taken those who see injustice being done to African Americans to ask what they can do. Meanwhile, there are people who continue to make excuses about why brutality is necessary. I mention these incidents of injustice, understanding that all police are not bad police. Even though one may have not walked in the shoes of racial injustice victims, many have and can resonate with some of the inhumane actions mentioned above.

The question is, what would you do if you ever experienced or witnessed someone close to you treated heartlessly because they are different? How about just speaking up and doing unto others as you would have them do unto you? There is a program on television, that is now in its fifteenth season called *What Would You Do?* [9] If you have not seen the show, I encourage you to look at it. Place yourself as an ordinary person who sees people behaving in a way that contradicts your beliefs and ask yourself how would you react. With that said, what can you do to mitigate racism and inequality within your circle of influence?

SCRIPTURE TO LIVE BY:

John 13:34

In the book of John 13:34, God commanded us to love one another, as He has loved us, so we must love one another. He also said, showing partiality in judging is not good. While finding solace in your studying of the Word, you may find that in His infinite grace and mercy, God will substitute for you a ram in the bush, rather than you sacrificing your integrity and sanity, just as He did in Genesis 22 with Abraham.

If you remember, a ram was substituted as a sacrifice, rather than Abraham sacrificing his only son, Isaac, by killing him. The ram in my situation was being asked to start and be a part of affinity/network groups in the workplace and having the opportunity to be in a capacity for being a trailblazer in various career positions and using my voice. Your ram may be something else. Just never stop looking for it.

Letter 4:
DEAR WOMEN WHO COMPARE YOURSELVES TO OTHERS

"For we dare not make ourselves of the number or compare ourselves with some that commend themselves; but they measuring themselves by themselves, and comparing themselves among themselves, are not wise" (2 Cor. 10:12 KJV).

How far back in time are you able to remember when you compared yourself to someone? When I was very young, I remember telling my mom that I wanted my feet to grow to the size of a playmate's who lived across the street from me. Everything about me was small, from my height, body structure, hands, feet, and so on.

When I shared my desire with my mom, her response was, "Why would you want feet that do not fit your body size?" This was her outside voice, and while thinking back on it, her inner voice probably thought, *poor child, why in the world would she want to have big feet?* I was smaller in stature than many kids in my age group, and I wanted to be their size.

Think about when you were around other children in your age group and there was something about them you admired or compared yourself to. You may have wanted long hair like theirs or to live in a home or have both parents in a household as they did. Now that you have matured, do you realize you may be continuing to compare yourself to others, making comparisons such as job titles, neighborhoods, car types, home size, their looks, income level, body type, hairstyles, hair length, hair color, clothes they wear, and so on.

Now, the social media frenzy has taken these comparisons to new levels. It is fascinating how we are more concerned about what other people are doing or how they respond to what we post than we are with the quality of our own lives or being in tune with our own mental and emotional state. What an addictive, time-consuming phenomenon!

Is it that we are concerned about them, or is all this comparison more about ourselves? I tend to think it is more about ourselves, and here is why. We evaluate others to measure our own abilities and opinions. Therefore, others are used as a point of reference to make a justifiable judgment of who we are, or sadly, we may even try to find our identity in who they are. Is what you see on social media really who they are, or is it a highlight of a point in time in their life that probably doesn't even always reflect their reality?

When you post, you post the good, not the ugly, unless it is about the passing of someone. Comparison is not always a bad thing, but it depends on the degree of self-assessment it may cause us to perform and our reasons behind it. Ruminate over your motivation behind self-comparisons. Is it for improvement, or are we looking for something to make us feel better or worse about ourselves?

Think about the deciding factors of who we are idolizing and coveting, and wonder at what point did we make that decision. At this time in your life, who are you choosing to compare yourself to? Think about how competing with this person or these people may or may not help you.

There were two things I compared myself with, and neither helped me in any way. Both created self-imposed barriers that prevented me from living my best life. My first conundrum was comparing myself to women who were engaged or already married. My heart's desire was to be blessed with a husband. Year after year, when it did not come to fruition, I became discouraged.

When confronted with challenges and not seeing my way out of them, eventually I would resort to the Word of God. The scripture, Psalm 37:4–5 came to mind which says, "Delight thyself also in the Lord, and He shall give thee the desires of your heart." This was not coming to pass for me. Then I would say, *Lord, if this is not your will, please take the desire away.* I continued to have the desire, and I continued to self-compare.

My second fixation was having to prove my value within a work environment. It was difficult seeing others excel, move to other divisions of the organization, and get promoted despite performing poorly or being involved in unethical activity. Witnessing this and knowing that if I had been involved in any of that illicit behavior, my days would have been numbered and that made my work life hard some days.

In my thirty-plus years in Corporate America, I grew to understand not only the culture but the politics, too. I mention this because when you have clarification on these two things, you have a better perspective on the organization's expectations and people's behavior. Understanding does not mean you like it, however, it's beneficial to your long-term success. Your understanding merely enables you to move forward with wisdom. Being in leadership roles in the past, I became troubled because I got a sense that the work I was doing was not good enough. I found myself in a vicious cycle of relentlessly trying to prove my self-worth to the business.

I've witnessed how leaders sabotage employees and have tried hard to circumvent this in my own career. This was the genesis of my decision to self-compare. There were times when I was micromanaged and criticized for the work I had done. In the eyes of my supervisor, not working ten to twelve hours a day meant I was not putting in the time to produce. When confronted in this way, one may start observing colleagues to see whether their work was being criticized also. You may discover that you didn't accomplish the goal in the same way, but the goal was accomplished nonetheless.

Yet, you continue to compare yourself to colleagues, working longer hours to compete and because you want to meet your supervisor's expectations. Eventually, you get promoted or transferred to another role or company. You can then finally take a deep breath, and be thankful that you've moved on from a taxing situation and leadership style, that is, until your breathing is stopped again in the next role.

Another illustration may be where you and your boss were peers initially, and shortly after, he or she became the person you reported to. Of course, the working relationship changed, but you did not expect it to be a competitive or envious relationship. Nevertheless, it triggered my endless comparison to others. My authenticity was diminished due to a competitive environment where a former peer became my boss. My true self was compromised because I felt a need to conform. It was like Dr. Jekyll and Mr. Hyde leadership.

It got to a point where I did not know what I was going to get from my boss on a daily basis. It should not have been about competition; it should have been about doing an effective job to deliver on the targets and goals of the position you are hired for. My demeanor would change around her in ways I shudder to recall. I would walk on eggshells, not knowing what to expect. My reaction reminded me of my backstory, having a critical mother and feeling like nothing I did pleased her.

Not witnessing my boss behave like this with my other colleagues, I became absorbed in meeting my supervisor's expectations. I would compare my peers' activities and outcomes to mine. I always wanted to do a good job because that was what I was paid for, whether satisfied with my pay or not. Again, if an employee is not performing to the expectation of the boss, the protocol is to let that employee know their performance was not meeting expectations. This protocol did not occur in my situation. So, the cycle of comparison continued, and I realized it had become part of my DNA (dominating natural ability), or my dominant personality trait. I wanted to stop this habit because it was becoming detrimental.

This is when you know there is a problem. There comes a point when you come to the realization that your authentic self is centered around stinking thinking: disappointment in yourself, lack of confidence in your abilities, being miserable, an inability to be your whole self, or low self-esteem. When this occurs, self-reflection surfaces. Are you able to trace comparing yourself to others back to childhood? If so, ponder whether you are just in your own way, or if you have been influenced by certain situations or messages that have become part of your belief system. We have clearly been influenced by messages, and now this is an opportunity to mitigate them, particularly if we realize it is not working for us. The key to this is first awareness, then face and admit your predicament, decide whether you want to stop, declare and decree you will, trust the process, and get ready for the journey.

KEY MESSAGE: Trust the Process of Change

Theodore Roosevelt made a good point when he stated, "Comparison is the thief of joy."[10] From my experience, joy is different than happy. Happy is a happening, an emotion where we may feel "contentment to bliss," yet it can leave you feeling empty, and it is a temporary emotion. Joy is internal, and it is not always a common feeling, but when it exists, you have a peace that will surpass all your understanding.

For me, the joy of the Lord is my strength, and there is a peace in knowing the joy I have did not come from the world; therefore, the world cannot take it away from me. You know how good you feel when you extend yourself to help someone else. Now, that is joy, and if comparison is the thief of joy, I don't want it. Trust the process through this journey to help mitigate self-im- posed barriers, and pray and ask God to help you. We have not, because we ask not. Commit to surrender to God's plan for your life fully.

We are our own worst critics. Our internal voice wreaks havoc at times, and we believe it, and then the focus is now on our weaknesses. When that happens, we usually do not have the capacity to be in the moment. While out and about, have you found yourself busy comparing yourself with people you are out with? Then you find yourself not enjoying yourself for obvious reasons. It reminds me of those in a big group consumed with selfies, so much so that they are not really *present* in the moment.

Let's flip the script and focus on our strengths, accomplishments, and what we are grateful for, rather than letting *our way* of comparisons get in our way to abundant living. Journal your accomplishments and what you are grateful for. Remember, there is always someone who wishes they were in your shoes. Like me wanting bigger feet as a kid, if I knew then what I know now, the size of my feet were just fine.

The meaning of expectations is "a strong belief that something will happen or be the case in the future." In other words, expectations that we have of ourselves tend to influence our reality to create results, and when they do not come to pass, we are disappointed. It can also be a motivator, knowing that there are some things we can control and others that we are not able to control. This is what I know.

- It does not make you feel better when you self-compare. It just kills your joy.
- Be careful when you choose who and what to idolize. Observe what this choice says about who you are.
- If your way of thinking about yourself and others is not cultivating your life, it's stifling your growth.
- Be intentional about overcoming illusions that stop you from learning and serving others.

SCRIPTURE TO LIVE BY:

2 Corinthians 10:5 KJV

Reset your expectations about who God created you to be, and exercise self-discipline. What a man thinketh is what he is. Second Corinthians 10:5 talks about casting down imaginations, thoughts, and suggestions that exalt itself against the knowledge of God, and bringing into captivity every thought. We must fight to maintain victory over our enemy.

Meditate on Philippians 4:8: KJV "Finally brethren, whatsoever things are true, whatsoever things are honest, good report, if there be any virtue, and there be any praise, think on these things." Compete only against yourself. Concentrate on how you will be the best you can be. Show up 100 percent and be competitive with yourself. Focus on the things and people that benefit you. Let's stop coming from a mind-set of lack. The world is plentiful, so it's time to believe.

Letter 5:
DEAR WOMEN WHO WEAR MASKS

"Jesus said unto him, Thou shalt love the Lord thy God with all thy heart, and with all thy soul and with all thy mind. This is the first and great commandment. And the second is like unto it, Thou shalt love thy neighbor as thyself." (Mathew 22:37–39 KJV)

When people talk about 20/20 vision, it is usually associated with having normal eyesight, and doctors determine this by how well your eyes can see an object at a distance of twenty feet. Now, when one thinks of or hears mention of 2020, the year that will always be remembered will likely come to mind, and not necessarily eyesight or perfect vision. That is because the year 2020 carries another connotation that is far from perfect. Categorized as quintessential, this was the year where lives and the world as they once were changed forever, and it was no longer business as usual.

A new normal was created in the year of the coronavirus pandemic, where certain precautions were mandated to mitigate the spread. For instance, wearing a mask; social distancing; business and school closings; state shutdowns; the reality of the number of deaths resulting from the virus, racism, injustice, and inequality exposed; and an unprecedented United States presidential election. In other words, 2020 is now associated with a history-making year that has impacted our country in profound ways.

Who knows, one day there may be a documentary called The Year of 2020 on Netflix that may include several series and episodes highlighting the mysterious unknowing of this era and how we were changed as a result. There may be some episodes that seem predictable and others you would find not only enlightening but insightful. Many people witnessed things they did not like; therefore, the question is what will we do about it? All who lived through 2020's events can choose to continue to be spectators, or in the words of Mahatma Gandhi, "Be the change you wish to see in the world."[11] In order to live the quote, it is imperative to bring your whole self to the table because you will be more effective in your gift and in fulfilling your purpose.

How ironic it is that wearing masks is a barrier to help prevent respiratory droplets from spreading onto other people, causing them harm. Figuratively, wearing one is also a barrier that prevents you from being your authentic self. Despite there being evidence supporting the efficacy of masks, there has been a lot of resistance to a point where people are saying or thinking it is their right to decide whether to wear one or not. Although it minimizes the spread of the disease, selfishness has taken precedence over being concerned or caring about others. What happened to civic duty or the Golden Rule to do unto others as you would have them do unto you? It seems it has become more about asserting your own rights than being concerned about the well-being of others.

There is a scripture that comes to mind, which reminds me to love my neighbor as I love myself. Maybe that is the key: loving yourself. Love is an action, but you may resist loving yourself or others because you simply do not know how. One may be so consumed with self that the energy or capacity to care about anyone else does not exist. Therefore, your true identity is often hidden by figuratively wearing a mask. Many have found that literally wearing a mask is uncomfortable, so imagine the impact of figuratively wearing one.

I have figuratively worn a mask more than I would like to admit. I had a need to protect my inner vulnerable self. Let me explain. Although it would have been more comfortable for me to have a child-like spirit by letting my hair down a bit in the corporate world. I felt I had to assert myself to be taken seriously. This was not my authentic self. I recall having a boss that would tell me to loosen up because he had noticed how much more fun I was outside of the office, and he thought that would be a great side to share with my colleagues and higher ups.

I was then made aware I had really been compromising my authenticity when I thought I was fitting in. We all wear masks for various reasons and agree to things for social conformity. We may attend a church because that is where we grew up, although it is not providing the spiritual food we need and desire. We hide our anxieties and depressive disorders for fear of being thought of as a psycho, smile because everyone else is smiling, and continue dating someone that we know is not good for us for fear we will be alone. Further, we openly agree with others when inwardly we do not agree, in order to avoid conflict. We pretend to be enjoying ourselves to conform with the crowd when we'd rather be home. In other words, we go along to get along.

The symptoms of the mask mentality can include difficulty in making decisions for fear of not being accepted and being afraid of making mistakes for fear of criticism. You may also have a distant demeanor for fear of being exposed as one who has been perpetrating a fraud, in other words, pretending to be someone you are not. Perhaps the most common and evident symptom of mask mentality brings the adage to life that hurting people hurt people, and the vicious cycle continues. What a stressful cycle that can be, living as an imposter.

KEY MESSAGE: Mask Mentality

The lesson I have learned from having a mask mentality are many, but here are a few based on what I know for sure and not what I have heard. Once you are made aware, you understand that figuratively wearing a mask is a "self-imposed" barrier preventing you from living your best life, and your 20/20 vision becomes a lot less clear. Eyes may be the window to your soul, but when the lower parts of your face are obscured, so are your emotions. This is what I know.

- Wearing masks has affected my interactions with people and opportunities by not being my authentic self.
- A mask makes me want to be accepted more than I want to be genuine.
- A mask makes me mute. I find myself not speaking my truth. The mask caused me to be stuck for fear of being criticized.
- The mask brings on physical and emotional illness because it's stressful trying to be something or someone you are not.
- Masks may cause you to look for love in all the wrong places.
- Wearing a mask every day affects your sense of self-esteem and worthiness.

Although the practice of wearing a mask during the pandemic was highly recommended, many found literally wearing a mask to be uncomfortable. Think about how difficult it was to identify people wearing one. You recognized some semblance of them and saw some spark of familiarity, but you were not sure and couldn't fully trust your judgment of whether it was really them.

How comforting it was when they finally snatched it off and unveiled their whole face and you could be confident in their identity, especially if you had let them in your personal space. It's also a relief for you when you can snatch off the figurative mask and bring out your whole self, being less guarded and more trusting. Imagine the impact of figuratively wearing a face mask, but presenting yourself to others every day, still expecting them to recognize the "real" you and welcome you in emotionally or professionally.

When you think of this comparison, it's not easy for the person wearing the mask and those expected to interact authentically with that one, acting as if this protective gear wasn't a barrier between them. Clearly, it prevents the real you from being exposed or embraced. In other words, it covers all the good stuff up, and none of us want that, do we?

I found a cheap silver ring online with an inscription that says, "You Are Enough." Not my usual style, but I felt compelled to purchase one for me and whomever God led me to gift it to. My beautiful, worthy sisters, the last thing that the mask mentality affects is your ability to see yourself in the image of God, your creator. It causes you to look for love in all the wrong places, as I did. You may go from relationship to relationship, presenting only a figment of your true essence. There is no freedom in hiding behind a mask, and it's not God's will for your life.

SCRIPTURE TO LIVE BY:

Psalm 139:14 (KJV)

The Word of God says you are fearfully and wonderfully made, marvelous are your works and your soul knows right well (Ps. 139:14). All of this says, you are enough, and the Word con- firms that you can trust it, trust yourself, and take it to the bank. So, walk in this with the confidence of Christ. Glory in it in your daily interactions. And pray for wisdom in how to change your thinking about who you are without the masks. Become yourself more each day.

Letter 6:
DEAR WOMEN WITH ESTEEM BATTLES

"For as he thinketh in his heart, so is he: Eat and drink, saith he to thee; But his heart is not with thee." (Prov. 23:7 KJV).

Wikipedia defines self-esteem as an individual's subjective evaluation of their own worth. When we diminish our own value, we lack self-respect, self-confidence, and self-worth. Perceiving ourselves negatively will affect many aspects of our experiences that prevent us from living our best life. It will have the propensity for some serious consequences, particularly if you do not meet your own standards or if our self-perspective is negative. Areas of significance would be our relationships, mental aptitude, and physical health.

The feelings of inadequacy will keep you stuck for fear you will either make a mistake, or you are not good enough or deserving enough. Although the Word of God tells us that "God has not given us a spirit of fear, but of love, power and a sound mind," there is a tendency when we carry the burden of low esteem to be super sensitive or assume the worse. Much of this often stems from our childhood. Whatever the adverse experience or the parenting style of whomever raised you, it can be overcome, but only if you so desire. There is also a flip side to low esteem.

God forbids us from holding ourselves with esteem that is too high or having high regard and admiration for ourselves, as opposed to humility. According to the *Read and Spell* blog, when comparing low and high self-esteem, both involve our thoughts and emotions and influences how we perceive others and interact with the world around us.[12]

During my childhood years as mentioned in Letter 1, "Dear Women in Your Own Way," our backstory has much to do with who we are today. My mother, although she wanted the best for me, was very critical by nature, and I found myself wanting to make sure what I did and how I looked pleased her. If one has experienced that type of scrutiny, you may have felt compelled to make sure all your bases were covered before entering that person's presence.

In order to avoid disparaging comments, you also may have become okay with having decisions made for you, as well as found a way to be okay with whatever comments were made about you. If this is the case, unfortunately during much of your life's journey you may have found yourself voiceless. Have you encountered someone who appeared to have always focused on the negative, rather than the positive things about you? If you have, did you start believing nothing you did or said was good enough?

Perhaps later in your life or now, you realized criticism pushed you to perpetual perfection mode. We all know that no one is perfect. What that does, if you do not perform to your self-made standards, is make you feel like a failure. Therefore, you may find yourself struggling to speak up because you feel you would be challenged. You may be unable to make your own choices because in the past, your decisions had been made for you. This causes you to not want to rock the boat, a desire to be liked, and being okay with going with the flow to stay within your comfort zone.

Studies have shown that parents or others who are heavy influencers in your life but extremely critical are likely the catalyst for one's low self-es- teem, but it does not have to be your end result. If your DNA (dominating natural ability) exudes lack of confidence, you may remain in the status quo pattern. For instance, you may stay in your comfort zone, not trying new things, and you may compare yourself to others, not experiencing life to the fullest. Instead, surround yourself with people who challenge you so that you can live to your full potential.

Keep in mind our lives have been shaped by our belief system. The way we think affects our character, conduct, and conversations. Our worthiness, as it relates to how we value ourselves as human beings, can also be tested by a life interruption. Do you believe two people can have the same things and live under similar circumstances, yet one is content, and the other is not? Absolutely, and this is because they both have different expectations and have exclusively measured their value by their self-standards.

Now don't get me wrong, it is good to have expectations and ways to measure your success in life, but not when it gets to a point where you are stalled and stuck from living your best life. If the majority of your time, you are operating with a lack of peace, this is a flag that something is beckoning for your attention other than what you were created to do. Pay close attention if you experience the following: irritability, carrying heavy burdens, experiencing self-destructive behavior, not indulging in self-care, depression, unworthy feelings, guilt, or you are a workaholic.

Let's take a deep dive into the effects self-esteem may have on relationships. First of all, man was not created to be alone, and I believe life would not be fulfilling without having relation- ships. I am talking about thriving, not just surviving. In other words, relationships are important, and it behooves those with esteem battles to gain clarity on how relationships play a significant role in our lives.

When one's perceptions are distorted, insecurities and self-defeating thoughts wreak havoc on your business, professional, and personal life. There are times when we all have experienced self-esteem challenges, but when lack of self-worth is constant, this can pose problems. When we are in a good place, have healthy self-esteem, are motivated, confident, and your authenticity (true self) reigns, it offers a segue to form deeper connections within our world and ultimately enhances your mental and physical well-being.

Once I became independent and had a good job, I was content. Then there came a point in time when I started envisioning myself with a husband and children and living in a home with a white picket fence around it. In the 1960s through 1970s era, women had been portrayed as homemakers, teachers, secretaries, and nurses. During these years, there were women who were becoming frustrated because they felt their ambitions were being neglected and replaced by their role as caregivers to their husbands and children.

With that said, the women's rights movement escalated, and the idea of women having the same equality as men was transitioning into more of a reality. Although I did not play a role in the movement, I did benefit from it. Having been hired in a management training program for one of the big three automobile industries was evidence of this. Despite the continued conflict about the roles women should play and how they should be valued, the program I was in was a stepping stone to be a manager for one of their satellite offices.

However, you know the saying, *you cannot teach an old dog new tricks*—humanity still holds tightly to how things used to be, and it has been difficult to change mind-sets, even in this day and time. While women and the workforce began to change dramatically, I continued to be fixated on having a husband and family and being a homemaker. The desire for this role continued to be significant for me, and perhaps the same is true for you.

Having grown up in a society where having a husband and family was the norm, when this was not becoming a reality for me. Therefore, I thought something was wrong with me. This feeling prevails, particularly when you are asked often, *when are you getting married?* Hearing this over and over intensifies the situation, and even more when it appears all of your friends and circle of influencers are marrying.

That can be yet another expectation that is not being met, so you may do everything in your power to make it happen. When this happens, you may find yourself "dating," or whatever you call it, and find yourself compromising your values in doing so. Despite your best efforts, you may not get the man who is best for you, and then you will attract who you have become, not what you have been created to be. While continuing to mature in age and yet not having been successful in finding that special someone, that can certainly influence your level of esteem and contentment.

Usually when you remain in undesirable situations like dating people who are not right for you, it diminishes your sense of self-respect and self-worth. This may be because you have settled, and you know within your heart of hearts that you have allowed yourself to indulge in a relationship that is not God's best for you.

If you were asked, "D*o you love yourself?"*, what would you say, and how would you qualify and or quantify whether you do or do not? Think about who you have a "strong affection for out of kinship or personal ties," and how you treat them. Is there a reason why you would not treat yourself as well as you would someone you dearly love?

KEY MESSAGE: We Grow from the Dark Places

Being in my own way for some years, initially I did not fully understand that esteem battles were an issue for me. I may have projected self-confidence, respect for myself, and even believed I loved myself. However, my actions displayed something different, so I could no longer ignore the impact low esteem was having on my inside. Professionally, being in environments with majority white men and attempting to convey my points in meetings, I found them basically saying the same thing I was.

However, folks seemed to listen to them but ignored me. As for the women, it was like a competition, yet we all were working toward the same goal. We were all looking for love, but most were looking for it in the wrong places. If one lacks self-worth, they may believe it can be found in other people or things, or both. If we have high self-esteem, our focus would be on growth and improvement, while low self-esteem focuses on self. What I know for sure from the lessons learned:

- Esteem is an inside job, not outside. Tell yourself good, positive things about yourself.
- Thrive, don't just survive. Be intentionally present in the moments that bring value to your life.
- Go to therapy! There is nothing to be ashamed of when there are professionals who can help.
- Take care of yourself and surround yourself with the right people, those who will speak life over you.
- Look for things to be thankful for and do things that bring you joy, including serving others.

We grow from the dark places of our lives, even as the enemy tries to make you think you have nothing to offer. Ask yourself what you bring to the table. What is it that you can make happen for yourself and others, and what makes your essence? Practice self-compassion and do something meaningful and fulfilling to boost your esteem and get rid of your self-imposed barriers.

SCRIPTURE TO LIVE BY:

Mark 12:30–31 (KJV)

If you witnessed the impact of a loved one's struggle with esteem challenges, what would you do? There is a scripture, Mark 12:30–31, which gives us the first and greatest commandment to love the Lord your God with all your heart, mind, body, and soul, and love your neighbor as yourself. Although self- love is a process, it is worth the work to begin elevating your self-esteem.

Because feelings change like the wind, I am not talking about the affections you have for someone else, but it's more about how good you feel about yourself. Love is an action, it's about the action steps taken to support the growth of our mind, body and soul. Once gratefulness and appreciation becomes a state of mind, your confidence, esteem and self-worth will take you places you may have thought were impossible.

Letter 7:
DEAR WOMEN WHO QUESTION WHETHER THERE IS A GOD

"But He said, you cannot see my face; for no one may see me and live"
(Exod. 33:20 NKJV).

When I accepted God as my Lord and Savior, things in my life got crazy, really crazy. This was confusing after hearing time after time that if I would turn my life over to God, as a follower of Jesus, my life would change for the better. Unfortunately, I did not find this to be the case in several instances throughout my life. You may have experienced after you accepted the call to give your life to Jesus Christ that major life challenges happened not too long afterward, and they may have kept coming vigorously.

Even though the message you may have heard on that day spoke directly to your circumstances, and you made the decision in that moment of time to surrender and to give your life to the Lord, challenges were ever present. You surrendered because you saw hope, and your faith became renewed. You were excited then and had an expectation that things in your life were going to be just fine. Suddenly, life happens again, and you realized you are not fully equipped. The education you gained did not offer you problem solving abilities, but God said He would give you life more abundantly. Yet, it seemed the abundant part was not happening. How confusing is that?

Maybe you found out you were pregnant out of wedlock and were not sure how you would handle it, or you or a close friend or family member received news of a cancer diagnosis. Perhaps you go to work one day to find your company has downsized, and you were left without a job like I was. Maybe your work atmosphere is stressful beyond your capacity, or you were smitten over a relationship only to discover he was dating someone else. I confess that was my modus operandi.

You may not be getting along with your boss and have started looking for another vocation but to no avail. Sometimes there's an inability to make ends meet, or you may find that you are living above your means. Imagine coming home one day and finding out either your mom, dad or sibling will not be coming home ever again, due to a death. For some, your home environment is in constant disarray because of alcoholism or drug addiction.

For me, I was always battling with health and emotional issues, like headaches, backaches, and even heartaches. I did not have problems going to see doctors, but what I did have problems with was always receiving the same diagnosis— stress. Also, within a short span, I lost two dear friends. One had AIDS and the other cancer, and both were young. For some reason, I thought if one had passed when they were older, it would have been more acceptable.

I was devastated, particularly because of the relationship they had with God, and both believed by faith that they would not die, but live. In retrospect, both lived longer than expected, and they continue to live in my heart. Needless to say, my heart was broken by the loss, and the pain hurt so badly that I wondered if I would ever get through it. This season in my life brought home the saying, "When it rains, it pours." It's like once you get over one thing, then something else happens to bring you to your wit's end.

As crazy as this may sound, my thinking was that if I relocated, it would be an opportunity to start my life over again. Have you thought about going somewhere where no one knows you to give yourself a clean slate to start over again? Once you realize the common denominator is *you,* you can become desperate for relief.

BUDDHIST FOR A YEAR

When one becomes vulnerable to the pains of life, we do many things to avoid and to eradicate the unbearable anxiety and angst. Although you accepted the call to give your life over to Jesus Christ, from your lens, life situations were not changing. In fact, emerging were different vices, such as alcohol, drugs, sex, gambling, shopping, binge eating, or becoming a workaholic. You believed at least one of these may be an alternative to fill an emptiness or void in your life. Before you know it, you have gained an emotional reliance combined with the physical to create some vices, which has caused you to be addicted.

Eventually the vices compound other issues in your life. There will be periods of time you will feel okay about your coping mechanisms, and you accept it as your reality until you discover the consequences of your actions are daunting. Vulnerability to pain can come in different forms. You may have heard the saying, *desperate people do desperate things.* When desperate for solace, you may be open to anything if you gain an emotional connection to something that is feeding the emptiness.

An example during one of my lowly periods, I reconnected with a friend who was visiting the DC area where I was living, only to find she had converted to Buddhism. Our time spent together made me realize how her life had turned around significantly since her conversion, and the peace and joy she exuded was certainly something I wanted. The irony of it all was that I had "witnessed" to her several years back about my relationship with God, and how good He was. I had witnessed to her time and time again throughout the years and asked her to consider accepting God as her Lord and Savior.

The last time I connected with her, I sensed the seeds I planted with her had taken root, and I was excited that she would be sharing testimonies with me in the future about the miracles God had performed in her life. Unbeknownst to me during this visit, I witnessed her temperament of joy and compassion and compared it to mine, and decided I wanted what she had. During our time together, she shared her Buddhist faith, and I attended a couple of Buddhist temples with her. Shortly after she left to return to her home, I committed to try the religion.

My first time walking in a Buddhist atmosphere was overwhelming, but I was happy to learn that the congregation was broken into welcoming small groups that met in various homes displaying Buddha shrines, rather than in the bigger temple with Chinese architecture. Some dressed like monks, but the most apparent thing was the sacred approach to worship and study. I dutifully meditated and chanted every morning and evening, kneeling on the floor with shoes off and burning fragrant incense. I was also fascinated by the testimonies, and despite my best efforts, I just couldn't really get into it or devoted to the faith.

She connected me with several people who believed in the tradition, and they assured her I would be in good hands. Needless to say, there was one request from them, which was not to attend my church for at least one year. They suggested I immerse myself with their tradition, because intermingling with two different beliefs would be confusing. That was prefaced by indicating if I was not comfortable with their beliefs, it would be okay to go back to my church. I concurred and began studying their materials and joining groups at different homes and chanting daily. I began to feel better, met lots of new people, yet there was something about what I was doing that made me very uncomfortable.

I was in a bittersweet situation, bitter about the mandate not to visit a church and sweet that I was open to experience a different tradition. However, the internal tug of war was like a spirit fighting with my flesh, and the spirit was winning. How I knew the spirit was winning is because when I made the decision to let go of the Buddhist tradition, I had a peace that surpassed all of my understanding. That was a case in point of having an emotional blind spot by not realizing the common denominator to all my life interruptions was *me*.

When we become desperate for relief, we begin looking for that relief in the wrong places, people, and things. Although the Buddhist path didn't work for me, I then realized and accepted *I* was at the core of my own demise, and I cried out for help. Keep in mind, when we were told to give our life to God, we believed things would change for the better. However, for many of us, it may appear things are getting worse, and you may doubt even whether there really is a God. I know I did, and this is what I did to test if God is real.

THE CHAIR

Feeling distraught while out one day, I felt like I was going to lose my mind. In a tizzy, it was time for me to have a come-to-Jesus meeting, and in that moment that meant I had to get home. I always wore a figurative mask in public, and the safest place to remove it was home. Knowing this was going to be a serious conversation with Jesus, the mask had to go. Once I arrived home, I ran up two flights of stairs, bawling my eyes out and screaming for help. I entered my dining room and abruptly pulled out a dining room chair and said, "*Look, God,* since You are so real, I want You to sit in this chair and prove it."

While still sobbing feverishly, I then began to share with Him all of my frustrations, past and present hurts, and what I expected when I accepted Him as my Lord and Savior and started going to church, reading the Bible, and attending Sunday school and Bible study. Then I said, "Did You hear me? If You are real, do something, like move this chair or at least say *something.* You said in John 10:10 that You died so that I could live life and live it more abundantly, and I am not having an abundant life. So, what's the deal?"

This monologue went on for a while, and suddenly I became so exhausted and had a terrible headache. I became weak and had to sit down for a moment when I realized He had not said a word and the chair had not moved. I then said to myself, *I knew He was not real.* I slowly got up, prepared something to eat, and looked at television for a little while. My energy level was depleted, so I decided to go to bed. I'm a person who sleeps on my side, and I recall being on my left side because I was facing the window in my bedroom.

I fell asleep and was awakened by a breeze blowing on my neck. I looked at the window, and it was closed. I then felt a presence in my bedroom. I literally felt something behind me, and then I felt something breathing on my back and hair. I was frozen and said to myself, *Somebody is in my house.* Specifically, I felt someone was in my bedroom and thought they were going to harm me. I was so afraid and wondered whether I was going to be killed. All of a sudden in my frozen state of mind, there was a calmness and the next thing I knew, it was morning. It was Sunday morning, so I got up and started my routine, which was to cook breakfast, get dressed, and go to church. In retrospect, I realized that I did not even think about my chair experience. I went to church, and the Word was powerful, yet I don't recall what it was about.

However, what I do remember was all of a sudden, I leaped out of my seat and started speaking in a language that I was not familiar with. I was speaking in *tongues,* and as hard as I tried to control myself, I could not. I then started running around the church like a crazy woman, and I heard my pastor say, "Let her go; leave her alone." Eventually I calmed down. Once I got myself together, I wanted to run out of the church because I was so embarrassed. What I did do was go to the back of the church and stood in the corner, and I looked around and said to myself, *What was that about?* I located a chair, pulled it to the back of the church and sat down. Boy, I was exhausted.

After church I ran to my car because I did not want to talk with anyone and did not want anyone to talk to me either. I usually mingle with church members, go visit, eat, go shopping, and so forth, but instead I went home because I literally had no strength. After being home, I reflected over my church experience, and suddenly I had an epiphany. My so-called come- to-Jesus meeting I experienced the day before came back to mind, along with knowing without a shadow of a doubt that somebody was in my room. I knew then, the breeze I felt on my neck in my bedroom the night before was the presence and movement of God. If I had seen His face, I would have had a heart attack. An audible voice impressed on my heart,

"Don't you ever test me again. Now *do you believe I am real?"* I then thought about how I asked Him the day before to prove to me whether He was real or not, and tears began to flow. Speaking in a language that was unfamiliar and running around on the inside of the church was certainly out of character for me. There was no doubt in my mind that He was real.

After the chair experience, I had a thirst for God like no other. I had this desire to get to *know* Him, not know *of* Him. He became my invisible friend, so talking with Him was a joy. I was on a quest to read the entire Bible, and I did. I could not get enough of Him. I would wake up with a spirit of expectation and retire for bed with an adrenaline high.

During those times, it was like my time had been redeemed. The more I spent time with Him, the more He would reveal himself by way of dreams, interventions, and visions that I know were undoubtedly from Him. My newfound relationship with God blew me away; I loved every bit of it. The peace, joy, and contentment I felt, despite distractions whirling all around me during that period of time, were priceless. That experience was the essence of surrendering to a relationship that one could not see and touch, yet it was an authentic experience like no other. This is my love story, a phenomenal first love that was so different than a natural love.

Although I doubted whether God was real, He continues to love me. The ability to see things from God's perspective will give us the strength to endure. Things happen based on plans for the whole, but we only see in part. It's like a puzzle, and in order for certain things to be accomplished or the whole puzzle put together, there are certain pieces that must be found and put into place first. It is not always about us, so being self-consumed does not help anyone and only hurts you in the end. If it were not for Donald Trump, Joe Biden and Kamala Harris would not have become president and vice president of the United States. Perhaps we would not have ever seen a woman vice president in our time.

Sometimes the Lord will bring turbulent times so we may fervently call on Him. When you lose a job, you appreciate the new job you get even more. Embrace your trials. This is not to say you will not be emotionally distraught in the moment, but if you are a believer, you know all will be well. Resistance is the cause of suffering, and criticism and judgment are forms of resistance. Suffering is never good, of course, but there can be some good that comes out of it. I may not know what peace is if I had not gone through turmoil.

When you have been through a storm, you will find yourself feeling more gratitude, kindness, and love. In the Word of God, the scripture reference in 1 Peter 4:12–13 states, "Think it not strange the fiery trials that will try you, as though some strange thing happened." Through this Word, God expresses to us that there will be interruptions of life, and we have a choice to either be bitter or better about them, knowing that either way, *stuff will happen.*

KEY MESSAGE: Stuff Will Happen, but He Is Real

I share that story, not because I want you to try what I did or to test God in any way for that matter, but just know that God will meet you where you are. He created you, therefore He knows everything about you, and if it takes your own version of the "chair experience" or trials and situations where God shows Himself to be real and faithful in your life for you to become a believer and give Him the glory, then so be it. This is what I know.

- When it rains, it may pour, but God will always show up and prove Himself faithful during your challenging times.
- God is *omnipresent,* meaning He is always everywhere at the same time. He's never far from you.
- God is *omniscient,* meaning He knows all and has every solution and miracle you will ever need in the palm of His hand.
- God is *omnipotent,* meaning He has unlimited power to do anything you need Him to do.
- Trials come to refine your faith!

God is real! And in the event you doubt that, ask Him to reveal Himself. You must be open to it, though. Gaining a relationship, not just religion, is the key. Seek and you will find, knock and the door will be opened, ask and it shall be given to you.

SCRIPTURE TO LIVE BY:

Acts 9:3-6 (KJV)

I was reminded of the conversion of Paul in the book of Acts, chapter nine, where Paul had journeyed to Damascus, and suddenly a light was shining around him from heaven. Paul then fell to the ground before hearing a voice ask, "Saul, Saul, why are you persecuting me?" Paul responded, "Who are you, Lord? What do you want me to do?" The Lord then told Paul to rise, go to the city and wait for instructions. Today, He is as real as He ever was, and God is commanding each of us to *arise, move, and wait* for His instruction for our lives.

Letter 8:
DEAR WOMEN WHO CARRY OLD SCARS AND RESENTMENTS

"When I walk into the thick of trouble, keep me alive in the angry turmoil. With one hand strike my foes, with your other hand save me. Finish what you started in me, God. Your love is eternal- don't quit on me now" (Ps. 138:7–8 MSG).

We all experience adversity and storms in our lives. There will always be occasions that bring pain, hurt, disappointment, anger, guilt, bitterness, suffering, fear, sadness, or loss. Causes are insurmountable, varying from divorce, loss of a loved one, childhood trauma, abuse, or illnesses. This letter is written in the context of past experiences that have not been dealt with. One may ask, *How would I know whether it has not been dealt with?*

And the reply would be to ask yourself this question: Is there any event that has happened in your life that evokes a feeling of discomfort or uneasiness? If this is the case, keep in mind external storms that lead to internal storms can affect you physically, emotionally, and mentally, causing us to start looking like what we have been through. An example might be running into a person who is around the same age as you, yet they look a lot older.

When getting older becomes noticeable, some people may say they are aging well or gracefully, or contrarily, they might assume the person has had a hard life. In other words, what's inside of you will come out, and potentially redefine how you look, think, and feel. Resentments and scars have the propensity to create your life experiences. If one has not acknowledged the root cause behind your angst and have chosen to avoid it, it is time to do so. If not, the scars and resentment can seep in and become detrimental to living your best life.

As I got older, I realized I resented my parents for not being truthful about my having a half-sister. I felt this way particularly because of the way it was revealed to me. When I was in elementary school, there was a girl who bullied me and made me feel uncomfortable. This persisted until she told me her mom suggested she should not treat me unkindly because I was her sister. Arriving home from school that day, I shared that incident with my mother, and she stated it was *not true*.

Despite my mom's response, during my first through twelfth grade school years, that story continued to be the buzz among other children and some friends of mine. This disclosure was shared with me at such an early age, as we were both just in first grade. Unfortunately, this did not set the stage for a relationship between us into adulthood. I used to wonder if there could have been a different outcome if it had been handled differently. But I once heard Oprah say that forgiveness is "giving up the hope that the past could have been any different,"[13] and I believe this is wisdom.

When you are at a young age, I don't believe some guardians or parents think about the impact of what they choose to share or withhold might have on a child or later on in life. This may be because the adults are dealing with their own demons and issues. One day, in retrospect, I resolved I did have a half-sister, based on snippets of some interactions I had with her throughout my school days, such as attending one of her birthday parties, my mother babysit- ting her one day, and the subtle behaviors noticed between our mothers when they were in each other's space. I was perplexed over how it all manifested, and why my mom, who I trusted, denied it, while others continued to expose it.

You, too, may have some resentment which may have been planted in your earlier life or which you experienced later in life. Regardless, more than likely, if you are not clear on the source of your pain, in addition to the impact it could have on your life, it may trigger trauma or drama and replay over and over in different life scenarios. There are times when we recognize there is a pattern to our madness, yet we keep repeating the same old stuff. The same old stuff could look like being in bad relationships, not being able to keep a job, continuous friction between you and your colleagues, not getting along with your boss, anger problems, having trouble with male or female authority figures, voicelessness, addictions, parent drama, or repeating the same mistakes in general, and so on.

These patterns could be a result of previous scars or pain and will repeat itself until we begin to heal. In other words, these cycles can go on and on, until you look up one day, and it appears life has passed you by. You will look back and realize you had become so consumed with the travesty of your life that there may have been some opportunities you missed or some dreams you did not pursue.

You may think to yourself, *Is this all there is to life?* As a matter of fact, you may resent what could have been. To avoid situations like these, acknowledge you are feeling resentment and identify patterns of your life that are unproductive or not moving you into a direction where you are living your life more abundantly. For me, I identified patterns of being in toxic relationships, and I became sick and tired of it and decided to do something about it.

I began to pray about my situation and sought counsel through therapy, knowing then it was still taboo to an extent. You were stereotyped back then if therapy was a route you wanted to pursue, and it was thought of as something you only did if something was mentally *wrong* with you. I realized something was wrong, and I decided not to be ashamed of that, although I remained discreet about whom I shared this information with.

What I discovered was that I was attracted to emotionally unavailable men because my father was emotionally unavailable. Remember, my mom was critical, and my dad was laid back, and I never confronted him about anything personal in his life the way I did my mom. The reason I did not use my voice with him is because I had learned that feelings were not expressed; they were only assumed. His demeanor never reflected strong emotions of any kind, whether happiness or sadness. And when I did approach him about something personal, his response was, "You deal with it and move on with your life."

Ironically, I was coined by many, categorizing me as being hard to read or figure out because I too was a bit expressionless. I have since grown to understand that lots of men do not easily express their feelings anyway. Although the men I dated looked different and had varied personalities, the pattern of being unavailable emotionally was evident. All of them had secrets, so I found it hard to trust them. In other words, I realized I attracted who I was. Remember, I did not acknowledge I had a half-sister because my parents never did. I was also emotionally unavailable, hard to figure out, and did not want anyone to get too close for fear of someone knowing more about me than I wanted them to know.

Some people may call this being aloof. If we do not acknowledge emotional scars, we will continue to have an internal injury, no different than if we had a physical injury that leaves a scar that remains for a lifetime. Although external physical or external scarring is more visible to others, do not underestimate the unseen emotional and mental scars. We must acknowledge the harm they can have on you internally, if they are not cared for, just like a scar that once bled and needed stitching. Yes, they too can be visible to others, based on your actions and behavior.

Keep in mind, how we think and feel creates your life experience. What I have learned for sure is if you do not understand the root cause behind the what, how, when, why, and where the scars and resentments originated, you will not be able to defeat them. An especially important caveat is forgiveness. Forgiving the person, people, or source behind the resentment is pivotal because if not, you will have lasting feelings of anger and bitterness internalized as unfair treatment. It will metastasize and spread like a cancer, and we all know the outcome of that.

Our bodies are not created to harbor long-term negative emotions that come from trauma and resentment. Emotions developed from scars of resentment can also pose health problems, such as headaches, anxiety, depression, high blood pressure, strokes, and many others. Imagine if you have any of these health problems. Wouldn't forgiveness be worth your complete and total healing from the inside out? Like my mom used to say, "If you do not have your health, you do not have anything."

KEY MESSAGE: Resentment and Unforgiveness Will Make You Sick

I am not saying the treatment, situations, or circum- stances you endured were not unfair, but what I am saying is we may never know why people do hurtful things to other people. Ironically, some are not even aware they have hurt you. Although we hear the saying, *hurting people, hurt people,* I can only surmise why my parents did not acknowledge their truth. Thinking about their childhood background, I know I can't judge them. Who am I to judge?

If it were not for my parents, I would not have accomplished what I have, and for sure, this book would not have been written. More importantly, they loved me to the core. We are so quick to say, "I would not have done what they did," yet we have not been in their shoes.

What I have concluded with my parents is they did the best they could with what they knew at the time. I know of women who have had four to five children, and they all had different fathers. I also know of women who have had three to four divorces. There is always a *reason.* If a person is satisfied with the trajectory of their lives, then that's okay too. Here's what I know:

- Childhood trauma and or drama in your life has to be recognized and dealt with.

- Repeating the same old mistakes or dysfunctions is a version of insanity.
- There is nothing wrong with admitting something is wrong and seeking professional help through therapy.
- Old scars don't have to leave a mark that are forever visible to others. Take care of your mental and emotional health.
- Forgive and be well. Unforgiveness and bitterness can make you physically sick.

Based on the personal stories I have shared throughout this book, I can relate to being a woman with old resentments and scars. Regarding my outlook back then on marriage, I was not comfortable and felt strongly there was more to life than what I was experiencing. This was driven by my heart's desire to have a lifetime partner. I know if we do not deal with scars and resentments, we will be stuck in a rut and will not live the full life we were created for.

We have choices, and we can choose to be bitter or better. I declare and decree for those who are engrossed in the pages of this book, you will choose better. It is not too late. I am not saying you will forget what has happened, but you will have to forgive.

Help Guide,[14] an independently funded nonprofit organization could not have described emotional trauma any better: "the result of extraordinarily stressful events that shatter your sense of security, making you feel helpless. It can leave you struggling with upsetting emotions, memories and anxiety that won't go away. Feelings that may leave you feeling overwhelmed. It is not the objective circumstances that determine whether an event is traumatic, but your *subjective emotional* experience of the event."

SCRIPTURE TO LIVE BY:
2 Corinthians 12:9 (KJV)

One of my favorite scriptures remind us that God's grace is sufficient, and His power is made perfect in our weakness (2 Cor. 12:9). So, no matter how much we have endured or how weak we may feel in our humanness, there is a power that God offers in His grace and mercy that rests on us. We still have to practice self-care to get better, but taking care of ourselves will be a process, and when you find yourself responding better to what had once triggered certain negative behaviors and you notice a real change in yourself, you will be so proud and will be on your way to living your best life. Trust me on this, if I can be delivered from this, so can you. The beauty of it is that I have become more aware of my fallacies, but now I know I have the choice to adjust to do something different. We will continue to be a work in progress, but we do not have to be who we once were. Hallelujah!

Letter 9:
DEAR WOMEN WITH PHYSICAL AND MENTAL HEALTH CHALLENGES

"Consider it a sheer gift, friends, when tests and challenges come at you from all sides. You know that under pressure, your faith-life is forced into the open and shows its true colors. So don't try to get out of anything prematurely. Let it do its work, so you become mature and well-developed, not deficient in any way" (James 1:2-4 MSG).

There is one person I know personally who had never had any physical ailments until her late seventies: my mother. I never witnessed any evidence of her having health challenges or being ill, but I do recall her always making a resounding comment: "If a person does not have their health, they do not have anything." It is not that I doubted or really understood that statement then; it just did not hold much credence until cancer, a virus, severe back pain, flu, and other medical diagnoses actually knocked on my door.

I preface with my mother not having health challenges, only because as I grew into adulthood, I had plenty. Let us keep in mind that health is defined as a condition of physical, mental, and social well-being. How many times have you gone to a doctor about a particular ailment and vital signs were taken, a litany of questions asked, examination given, blood work ordered and perhaps a specialist referral given? After all of that, the diagnosis was either stress related, or they were unable to find anything. You then think to yourself: *If I hear the culprit is stress one more time, I am going to scream.*

In other words, hearing that you are stressed and being told you must find ways to destress will make you even more tense. Then I started feeling bad about being stressed. Is it because we do not identify stress as a catalyst for illness or see it as a tangible symptom? This is something we can't afford to take lightly or overlook. Stress triggers a combination of signals from both hormones and nerves. These signals cause your adrenal glands to release hormones, including adrenaline and cortisol. As a result, stress becomes an emotional and physical strain on the body, and it basically comes from an uneasiness and how we react to challenging situations that occur in our lives.

There is no way around having turbulent times in our lives. Many of us have heard the adage, "It's not what happens to you but how you react to it that matters." Here is another one, "Life is ten percent what happens to you and ninety percent how you react to it." We may agree and have a glimmer of hope for ourselves and others to overcome these life challenges, despite our obstacles. It certainly does something to your psyche when things happen to you like the passing of a loved one, constant violence in your neighborhood, or unemployment. The same is true for unmet expectations at a certain age in life, broken relationships, being molested, divorce, long- term physical health conditions, or the diagnosis of an illness.

There are countless other examples of what some may call life interruptions. When trials come, reflect on your action or response for a minute. I am certain you will have multiple and sometimes competing emotions. Our thoughts not only create how we feel, but how we behave too. In other words, our beliefs about our situation *and* feelings about it can raise our stress levels. Although our bodies are designed to experience stress, we must be cognizant of the type of stress that's being felt; is it positive stress, like being promoted or getting married; or is it negative stress, as in the passing of a loved one, being abused, or overwhelmed with work? If there is a constant feeling of stress, it *will* impact your health if it is not addressed.

Let me provide another iteration. When stress is produced, it does two things. Number one, it helps us avoid danger, such as a perceived threat. For example, if you were in a pool and you accidently slipped in the deep water or are in a near car accident. Number two, stress can cause danger to our bodies if we are constantly worrying about what we cannot control. A prime example of negative stress happened while on my corporate job. Whatever position I held, my goal was always upward mobility, so being stagnant in a role was not an option.

Needless to say, accomplishing this goal took a lot of hard work, which included long hours. Perhaps you are a person who does a great job in setting those boundaries around your workload, without sacrificing family, friends, or personal time. Has work and life balance been questionable in your life, and have you struggled from time to time with how to obtain it? Maybe your hard work has been more about trying to demonstrate your worth, which may cause you to say that there are not enough hours in a day. When those thoughts become your focus, it's time for a mental shift. Unfortunately, I did not know at the time how to do that.

Humans Are Not Machines

I found myself becoming a working machine as opposed to a healthy, happy, well-balanced human being. When we are exhausted, our bodies produce more cortisol, a stress hormone. I found myself always having doctor's appointments, and the diagnosis was stress, or nothing in particular was diagnosed. I struggled with this because I really had stomach pain and headaches that were becoming unbearable. Not realizing that humans are not machines, little 'ole me, however, kept pushing forward, and my drive was like a hamster that was not able to get off the wheel. And I did not know how to control it. If only I knew then that this would be the beginning of my physical and mental struggles.

My intent of this letter, ladies, is to highlight the chemical changes stress causes in our bodies that may lead to raised heart rate, high blood pressure, upset stomach, headaches, and so on. In other words, it can be detrimental and if not managed appropriately, it can kill you. An astounding statistic by WebMD cites, "Seventy-five to ninety percent of all doctor's office visits are for stress-related ailments and complaints."[15] Imagine, these are people who actually go to a doctor, so think about many who do not see a physician.

Earlier, I emphasized health being defined as a condition of overall physical and mental well-being. In reference to mental health, the effects of prolonged stress can include anxiety, depression, irritability, moodiness, procrastination, low energy, and lack of concentration and motivation. Imagine the impact these effects may also have on a person physically and socially. For me, I had headaches and stomachaches, and on the social end, I always placed my work before my family, friends, and playtime.

Let's consider another aspect of your life. In the *Forrest Gump* movie of 1994, Forrest quoted his mom saying, "Life is like a box of chocolates,"[16] which alludes to life being the same as not knowing what you will get or bite into next with a box of mixed chocolates. You may have bitten in a piece of "life" chocolate to find yourself experiencing periods of being in a funk, feeling sad, depressed, lonely, dismayed, or even hopeless. If so, were there certain seasons of the year when you felt this way, such as a holiday or in the wintertime, or did it have something to do with an event that may have occurred during one of those times? Sometimes you may not even know why you are feeling as you do. It could be temporary or long lasting.

Whatever it is, it is not a comfortable place to be. I must confess, when I have experienced these emotions, I always felt if I could clearly answer *what, why, and how,* I could make sense of it all and would have a sliver of relief. So, in other words, it's important to have answers, especially related to things that make you uncomfortable and impact your quality of your life.

Cause for Alarm?

When you are out of your funk, there is a sense of reprieve; however, it may keep coming back from time to time, and you realize the bouts are lasting longer each time. If this is the case, one might assume there is a cause for alarm. When this happens, it is imperative not to diminish those feelings and know you are not alone. Seek support in managing your emotional health. Once I sought help, it was determined that my solemn mood was caused by depression. If you have been diagnosed with depression, anxiety, or a different mental illness, you may have thought you were impaired before in your daily life activities, but the diagnosis alone may take you over the edge. If you have the same fallacies as I did, it will be difficult for you to conceptually get it to make sense.

You may question whether it is genetic, what people will think about you, whether you are going to be okay, and if you will make it through this. You may also wonder why it is happening to you, although you still have so much to be grateful for. You will even second guess why you are feeling this way and whether it is a curse. Finally, if you have a relationship with God, you may cry out and ask how this could be, saying "*Lord, help me.*" There may be times you question your very existence. You can become so ashamed; you start cutting yourself off from people, and isolation is the worst thing you can do.

There was an incident during my journey where I com- mitted to let someone stay with me for a while if she fell on hard times. When I told her this, I sincerely meant it, but unbeknownst to us both, she actually did fall on hard times. Unfortunately, it happened during the timeframe when I was consumed with depression. I could not possibly let her see me in the condition I was in because I was ashamed.

At this point and time in my life, my only regret was not being mentally available to be there for her when she needed me most. Perhaps one day, God may allow me the opportunity to redeem myself and apologize to her. Now that I know my diagnosis, I can defeat it with the help of God.

Another important factor, regardless of what type of stress you are under, we cannot overlook the significant role our hormones play in our overall physical and mental health. Stress triggers a change in the serum level with the following hormones: cortisol, catecholamines, and thyroid, as studied and revealed by Mayo Clinic.[17] However, the primary stress hormone is called cortisol, which functions in a certain part of our brain and manages our behaviors, motivation, and fears.

Keeping in mind my physical and mental health challenges experienced throughout my life, I feel blessed to share my story with you today, particularly because I was able to endure it only by the grace of God. I know my trials and tribulations have helped others, and I have not been placed on this Earth just for myself. One of my mantras is: "You cannot tell me any- thing if you have not experienced it yourself."

Although the body is complicated and depression, mental illness, and anxiety are complex, I continue to be in awe about the facets of our bodies. It amazes me how our endocrine system is made up of glands. These glands are where hormones are produced, stored, and released, sending messages and information from one set of cells to another. From there it travels through our organs, bloodstream, and tissues. In other words, when our bodies receive stress, our adrenal gland releases the cortisol hormone to our blood stream. It is doing what it is supposed to do, and it is our natural fight-or- flight response.

Once our stress level is under control, the cortisol hormone goes back to normal. When thyroid function slows during stress, it can also play a part in your emotional state, as it, too, can cause a decrease in hormone levels and issues balancing blood sugar. So, being under constant stress can wreak havoc on our bodies. It can also increase the risk of anxiety, heart disease, obesity, chronic pain, and depression. I have met a couple of people in my lifetime who suffer with chronic pain, and I know how debilitating that can be. For a year, I suffered from lower back pain that was so unbearable that I eventually had to take leave from work.

I went to countless doctors, and I recall going to a pain specialist. He was the only doctor who provided some relief until one day he performed a procedure on my back while I was under anesthesia, When I woke up, I was paralyzed from my waist down. To make a long story short, I gained consciousness seven to eight hours later, and I was diagnosed with degenerative disc disease in L4 and L5, along with scoliosis.

This came at a time in my career where I continued working as a human machine, not a human being. We know stress can affect or cause behaviors, such as excess drinking and smoking, which ultimately causes additional health issues. I thought about drinking during recovery from this procedure, but I was dealing with enough, so thank God this was not the route I chose for me or that God allowed.

The Power of Hormones

A high concentration of estrogen in a woman's body can increase cortisol levels as well. Although it's called the stress hormone, cortisone is a steroid hormone produced in the adrenal gland and is about more than just stress. Cortisol is also used in the body for blood sugar and metabolism regulation, inflammation reduction, and memory formulation. So, having high levels of this hormone in your system over an extended period, if unmanaged, may have lasting negative health effects, including belly fat, high blood pressure, fatigue, lack of focus, and irritability.

Let me offer one more validation of the power of our hormones. Estrogen levels increase during pregnancy and reach its peak during the third trimester. Ladies, we were created to have a baby, which means we are equipped with all the physical and emotional ingredients we need to give birth; however, most of us are aware that post- partum depression can follow this beautiful life event. This is normal and usually won't last. Considering all the above mentioned, we cannot negate the power hormones play in our lives or its contribution to our emotional health. I encourage you to consider having your hormone levels checked from time to time.

There is no scientific evidence that stress alone causes early menopause even though the symptoms of stress and menopause are similar. I firmly believe that stress was the cause of the start of my early menopause in my mid-thirties. Worry happens in your mind, stress happens in your body, and anxiety manifests in both. Are you a silent stressor, a person who, when others see you, it appears you have it all together? You may be well studied and exude confidence and strength, and some women in your circle may even aspire to be like you because you're perceived as being at the top of your game. All that is great, but keep in mind we are not super women. If you are a silent stressor and it is constant, do not ignore it. This can be no different than a closet drinker, gambler, or other kind of addict. I use these examples because people often can better relate to these common vices. Often depression and anxiety have been hidden struggles in our society and have slowly been accepted as just another disease. By putting it in the forefront in a way that makes it relatable, I am hoping it changes the stigma, so people are more open to talk about it and get the help they need.

What I experienced was frequent headaches, backaches, stomach problems, high blood pressure, depression, a few episodes of anxiety, and early menopause. None of it was enjoy- able. There were times, I was off the charts both physically and emotionally. If you experience any of those symptoms constantly, be thankful there is now a mental health platform. It is a shame so many are still suffering in silence. Take advantage of the mental health hotline, National Alliance on Mental Illness, counseling by online chat, national suicide hotline, holistic telehealth, peer-to-peer support, or an experienced counselor, therapist, or psychiatrist.

Trust me, you are not alone. An article written by Robert Porter and medically reviewed by Lauren Fawley states that as of June 2020, there were an estimated 300 million people around the world suffering from some type of mental illness. [18] Pew research reported that in 2019 there was a significant increase to 28 percent from a relatively stable 22 percent of individuals seeking information on mental health. Today, there has been a 30 to 40 percent increase of people seeking help, which we understand could be attributed to the COVID-19 pandemic.

My mom's statement holds a lot of credence today. I now better understand the adage, *if you do not have your health, you do not have anything.* If you are not clear about what you want, because you are so busy hiding behind what you *don't* want, it robs us of the energy needed to tap into what we really want. When this happens, the enemy's mission is accomplished, and you are not able to be the person God intended for you to be. I believe the enemy fights you harder to stop you from doing what you were born to do, including building the body of Christ. There are now plenty of tools and resources to mitigate the barriers of health challenges so you can live your best life.

KEY MESSAGE: Listen to Your Body and Trust God

Set boundaries that are least resistant to burnout, so you can protect yourself by placing safeguards around your mental, physical, and social well-being. I will never know whether my mental challenges were genetic or hormonal, but what is more important is that it allowed me to become more educated on the power of hormones and how they play a significant role and has allowed me to learn, grow, and serve others who are confronted with this test.

We all are dangling on a string, so we cannot let go of God or give up on ourselves or one another because God does not want us to fall. My doctors have shared with me that depression gets worse with each bout. That was enough to scare the hell out of me. For me, depression is like a thorn in my side, as illustrated by Paul in 2

Corinthians 12:7. We may not know what type of thorn that was in his side, but I know metaphorically the thorn in my side is mental stability. When I hear of the different mental illnesses or teenagers committing suicide, I can relate. Since we all will be faced with trials and tribulations, you will not be given a choice of what your thorn will be. Think about it. Even if you were given a say, how could you ever choose?

I've surmised the best way for God to complete a good work in you is in your valleys of hardship. Look for different scriptures that will anchor you in time of trouble. What I know for sure is God had to allow a lot to happen to me before He could do anything through me, and you are no different. What touches you emotionally will change you to be bitter or better, so choose better because you will not be disappointed.

The only way physical or mental health will hinder you from fully serving God is if you do not ask Him to help. Seek and you shall find, ask and it shall be given to you, and knock because the door will be opened. Work on *not* taking the path of least resistance because you will find light at the end of the tunnel. Here's what I know.

- Take care of yourself because no one else will.
- Get your hormone levels checked as regularly as necessary, based on your symptoms.
- When you are confronted with trials and tribulations, pray about everything, and worry about nothing.
- You may not have all the answers regarding the burden of your physical and emotional health, but just embrace and trust God.
- Relieve stress in your life with activities, such as prayer, diet and exercise, meditation, yoga/pilates, journaling, therapy, and pets.

- Choose healthy relationships that are both good *to* you and *for* you.
- Have conversations about your physical and mental challenges with people you trust.
- Journal about your journey of your physical and mental challenges.

Change your perspective about why you have been challenged with physical and mental challenges. Perhaps it is for someone else, and if you can serve others by sharing your journey, it will be worth it.

SCRIPTURE TO LIVE BY:
James 1:2-4 (MSG)

The Holy Word reminds us in James 1:2–4 (MSG) that it is a gift when tests and challenges come at you from all sides. Yes, you read correctly, a *gift*. The explanation it gives is that under this tremendous pressure, our faith-life is forced to reveal itself in the open. Finally, the scripture warns us not to try to skirt or get around this fate when it's your turn because this is how you mature and become well developed and not lacking in any way.

When you are confronted with physical or a mental illness, process it in your mind, but do not be succumbed by it; instead seek help. Talking to people who love us and have our best interest at heart is good also. Who knows, they may be the ones to direct you to needed resources.

Prior to making any moves, pray about your situation, and ask God to lead you to the right people. Ask God to reveal and give you an understanding of His Word. What I learned is any earthly wisdom I may have about my situation does not compare to what God will reveal and has in store for me. I now fully embrace that this trial has enabled me to develop strength, increase my faith in God, and develop my character.

It has helped me to recognize the value and power of the human mind and body. Both are to be taken care of. These challenges have taken me to spiritual places I would not have ordinarily gone on my own. More importantly, it is by God's grace that I am still here. With that said, let God do His work so we can become mature and well-developed, not deficient in any way. I promise, you will have unspeakable joy more often in your life.

Letter 10:
DEAR WOMEN WHO HAVE LOST A LOVED ONE

"There is a time for everything, and a season for every activity under the heavens; a time to be born and a time to die. A time to weep and a time to laugh, A time to mourn and a time to dance." (Eccles. 3: 1–2, 4 NIV).

When sharing my thoughts with a few people about writing this letter to you, their response was as I had expected. The retort was as follows: *Really? Why? It is not much you can say about losing a loved one, and do you think the timing is right, based on the outcome of the pandemic our country has faced?* I should have known better than to divulge my thoughts—until it dawned on me that I was seeking approval because that is part of my backstory. When you feel severely or frequently criticized by a close relative or immediate family member like I felt from my mom, the impacts as an adult could be, among other things, a desire to seek approval and affirmation from others.

We know how easily criticism and naysayers can be an obstacle course to mitigate our initial intentions. That is what we call a self-imposed barrier, and what an opportune time to ask yourself: *Is my way in my way?* In my case, the answer was, absolutely, because this self-doubt had me question what I believed God placed on my heart to do. Being in my own way had nearly won until I then decided that if this was something God impressed upon my heart to do, then so be it. You are witnessing the evidence of my obedience by writing this letter to you.

It appeared in 2020 that most of us were forced to develop an intimate relationship with loss and tragedy of various magnitudes. We lamented and grieved the passing of loved ones, colleagues, or friends, some gone too soon. Whether through the throes of COVID-19 or some other traumatic happening, death felt imminent and persistent. It was all around us, in mass media, and in every conversation. Even if it was as simple as mourning the loss of what used to be, grief was a constant companion during the year none of us will soon forget. In growing up, the thought of losing a loved one was fleeting.

You may have heard your parents or people in your circle of influence discussing a neighbor or someone they knew who had died. The way you may have seen them show their respect and caring was by collecting money from neighbors to provide the bereaved family with expressions of love, such as flowers, cards, cash, food, or attending their memorial service.

Witnessing the grieving process then may not have been a dominant factor from your point of view because it did not impact your heart. When you do not have skin in the game emotionally, it is not that one does not care, the impact is just not strong enough to conjure up any strong, crippling emotion. In other words, we are familiar with the probability of death until losing someone close becomes your raw reality.

If we live long enough, we all will grieve over someone at some time in our life. Only those of you who have lost a loved one knows what this is like, and I know for sure you experienced an assortment of emotions. One thing for sure, although no one can predict their future, there is one guarantee, and that is we all are going to die one day. Whether we lost a loved one suddenly, by violence, tragically, or through an illness, it is something to behold, but the grip does loosen over time.

One is never ready for it, and whether it happens unexpectedly or not, all I can say is, oh my God, brace yourself. It is never a comfortable experience, in fact, it's heart wrenching. My first experience of losing a loved one was with a colleague who died in his early to mid-thirties from AIDS. There was so much ambiguity around the disease during that timeframe, yet I had grown to love him immensely. I was moved by the authenticity he had with me and his love of life because it was a rare quality in a corporate environment.

For me, he was the real deal and fun to be around, and I guess due to the fondness I had for him, I was baffled over the fact folks were more focused on the cause of his death rather than genuinely caring for the whole person. I recall the last time we spoke; he was in the hospital and asked me to pray for him. His request made me uncomfortable because during this phase of my life, prayer for someone on their death bed was unfamiliar and there was a fear of the unknown. I had no idea what or how to pray under these circumstances. I then suggested someone else I felt was more suited. He emphatically said, "No, I want you." I avoided his appeal, until I arrived home and could not shake his request from my heart.

Have you experienced getting a request from a loved one before their death and not honoring it? You may personally have requests you would like for your end of life, and instructions for after your transition, and perhaps no one knows what they are. Most of the time, many of us do not know what our loved one's desire is when entering the last stages of their lives. A couple of days later, I returned to the hospital to pray for him to find he was in ICU and unconscious, but I prayed for him anyway. I heard as people are transitioning, the last thing to go is their hearing. By God's grace and mercy, I honored his request, and I believe he heard me. I was devastated when he passed away, and that was the start of my raw reality with the death of a loved one.

No matter your age, your parents or loved ones are still aging. Some of our parents have reached an age where "the talk" is necessary. I would say it's unavoidable; if so, many of us didn't find a million ways to do just that: *avoid.* Discussing the end of life or death has to be the most difficult conversation to have. It's understandable, since mortality is not some- thing folks like to talk about. And it's not just talking to your relatives and friends about their end of life wishes, but what about you expressing your own wishes? Does *not* having that talk mean we are avoiding something? If that be the case, take a deep dive into your consciousness to figure out why you are avoiding the discussion.

When your children were born, I will bet you spent the majority of the nine months planning and preparing for their birth. Likewise, we spend at least one year planning our wed- ding. Ironically, even with knowing our life will one day end, we do not want to spend a mere few hours preparing a plan for that inevitable day. Our avoidance has become obvious. A study done by Pew Research in 2006 [19] shows where only one-third of adults prepare an advance directive, which as defined by *Webster's Dictionary* is a written statement of a person's wishes regarding medical treatment, often including a living will.

This document ensures those wishes are carried out should the person be unable to communicate them to a doctor. It also includes the person's wishes for what to do with their body after death. We can only imagine the dismal percentages for end-of-life planning even beyond the advance directive. Let's reframe the term to advance planning, since the term end-of-life may be too ambiguous. Advance directive and planning encompass medical decisions, insurance policies, inheritances, finances, funeral wishes, and legal power of attorney, a document giving a person the ability to act on one's behalf, and more.

Perhaps proactively discussing advance planning for your loved one or yourself, is a more straightforward way of learning and documenting wishes and values, rather than being reactive when something does happen. Even though some people may have different views and perspectives, it is simply not wise to wait before discussing, or to keep putting off initiating a plan. Baby steps can be taken, but to even start the process is progress. What a blessing it was for me to have done advance planning with my parents. Knowing their deaths are inevitable, as is mine, I could not imagine living life without them while at the same time having to take care of their end-of-life wishes without their directive.

God only knew they would live long enough, whereas the probability of medical treatment having to be decided would be a reality. Being allowed to be more focused on what their wishes were provided solace for me, knowing I would be able to honor them. What a surreal experience when I was present during my dad's transition. Although I will always miss my dad, I knew I had done the best I knew how with all the information I was provided, which gave me a peace about laying him to rest. I am compelled to reiterate that it is critical that you get your and your loved one's business in order, and make sure the appropriate people know the details of yours and their directives and final wishes.

Do you really believe it is okay not to talk about some- thing inevitable for each of us? Were you taught the subject is taboo? Is it the culture we live in, or better yet, do you work best in a crisis mode? When we do not have the conversation, the outcome will be overwhelming and stressful. Whether we are swift to admit it or not, family conflict surfaces, particularly when a parent and or relative dies and there are assets involved. Not only do you have to cope with the death of a loved one, now your family support system is the epitome of dysfunction at its worst.

Also, avoiding advance planning places an additional emotional toll on you when your loved one passes away. Whether or not you feel you have made the right decisions regarding the care your loved one received at the end of their life, not knowing for sure due to lack of clear direction from them can still prick at your emotions during such a vulnerable time. Having opposing family input on what should be done with your loved one usually does not end well.

The grieving stages alone are a lot for a person: denial, anger, bargaining, depression, and acceptance. So, why not take care of things you can control. If you love someone, knowing love is an action word, have the conversation, and execute the advance plan with peace of mind.

KEY MESSAGE: Life Is Short

The adage, *life is too short,* is not a cliché. It's a fact and 100 percent true. When you think about the average life expectancy in the US being 77.8 years old in 2020, and that number "declined by 1.0% from 78.8 in 2019"[20] the nearly eight decades most of us get on this Earth really is fleeting, and indeed, *too short.*

One day we are graduating from high school, and in the next blink of an eye, we are a parent then grandparent watching through tears as our children and grand- children graduate. I remember like it was yesterday, sitting in my apartment living room with a financial planner as a twenty-five-year-old professional. She was much older than I was, and I respected what she was sharing. She looked me square in the eye and walked through a retirement and investment plan, starting with the simple question, "At what age do you plan to retire,[21] and how much money do you think you will need to live comfortably?"

I was only a few years out of college and remember thinking that these were silly questions at my age and also feeling like I had all the time in the world. I did listen that day, but I did not act on it immediately. Eventually, I did act and was able to meet my retirement age goal of fifty-five. Like me, you may not act today, but I pray you will before it's too late. We are all going to die, and in John 10:10, we are told that the enemy comes only to kill, steal and destroy, but God came that we may live life more abundantly.

Living more abundantly in this situation means controlling what you can control. We don't know the time nor the hour that death will come. However, we can control how proactive we are in planning for ourselves and those we love. You are well aware of your family dynamics, so don't put yourself in the way of their turmoil or in your own way by not having a clearly defined advance plan from your loved one. Here's what I know.

- Death is inevitable, so don't let yourself be caught without a plan.
- Emotional chaos and devastation happens during loss of life. Let your proactivity be the calm in the storm.
- Planning brings peace. You won't be sorry you did.
- Difficult conversations don't have to be. Just sit down, ask questions, get answers and execute the plan. Just do it!

SCRIPTURES TO LIVE BY:

Ecclesiastes 3:1, 4–5 (NIV)
Mark 14:32–42 (NIV)

We live in a world of constant changes. The NIV Matthew Henry Commentary translation of Ecclesiastes 3:1, 4–5 says, "The different events of time, and condition of human life are vastly different from one another, and we are continually passing and repassing between them." What is constant is that if we are born, we will die. Let me correlate this with Jesus's birth and death. Jesus was born to be placed in the world as a human being so that He would be able to identify the experiences of humanity and to die on the cross for our sins. Undoubtedly, He understood the battles we have within our spirit, controlled by the desires of the Spirit and our flesh, known as our sin nature.

The NIV translation of Mark 14:32–42 explains that when it was time for Him to die, He agonized over God's will for Him. He wanted to come up with alternative ways to save the world without having to suffer and submit to God's will. Sound familiar? Every purpose has its time, so some of the seasons we find ourselves in are purely from God, and others depend on our will. Although we are not able to stop ourselves from dying, nor the grief that will go along with it, we have the ability to "advance plan" to mitigate barriers, self-imposed, legal, and others.

Life is complicated enough, but what a blessed assurance that we will laugh and dance again. If you have ever been delivered from a jacked-up season or made it through grief or mourning, how could you not want to serve God, our Father, with joy and gladness in your heart, while you still have breath in your body to do so.

Letter 11:
DEAR WOMEN WHO ARE CONFUSED ABOUT YOUR PURPOSE

*"Where there is no **vision**, the people **perish**: but he that keepeth the law, happy is he"* (Prov. 29:18 KJV).

A woman named Nicole Johnson has a powerful skit on video called "The Invisible Woman," which can be found on YouTube[22]. She makes a compelling indictment on women

in every society around the globe who may feel invisible in the lack of value placed on their contribution to society and some- times in their own homes and communities. She is dressed in all black with a black background and begins the skit by relaying when "feeling invisible" first began for her, which was walking in a room in her own house and speaking to her children, only for her exclamations or requests to them to seemingly fall on deaf ears.

She describes eventually experiencing the same at various social outings, where she would speak and no one seemed to hear or see her. At that point, she questioned her purpose for existing. Can you relate? Many of us can, as it can sometimes be a journey for some to uncover God's pre-ordained purpose for our lives and our existence on this Earth.

There are so many of us consumed with questioning what we should be doing or offering the world. Oftentimes, we may forget to be fully present in the moment and truly value our- selves for whatever it is that we contribute. Nicole Johnson felt this way, too, until a friend gave her a book on the great cathedrals of Europe with the inscription, "With admiration for what you are building when no one sees." She felt that her contributions as mother and wife were insignificant and often unnoticed. The book she was given was filled with completed cathedrals, which some took over 100 years to build.

They were built by artists and workmen who worked tirelessly and with skill day after day over many years to build these massive works of art that most would never see finished in their life- time and that they would never get to live in or see their name on. The point she made in conclusion of the video is that it's okay if no one sees your sweat or gives you accolades for doing a great job because no sacrifice is too small for God to notice. She went on to say that He smiles at every task done in love and excellence, every costume sewn, or sandwich made.

She reminds us that we are all building great cathedrals of our own, big or small, and the only one who matters if they recognize our work is Almighty God. Knowing or finding your purpose works the same way. It's a God thing, and His approval is the only thing that matters. There is no big purpose versus little purpose, and one person's calling or gift is no less significant than another's. It took me some time with God, but I am clear that my purpose is to empower women to be the best they can be.

I used to regret the many years I wore a mask, even when being called on to sacrificially help others. Now I see that I was hidden. Thankfully, I have reemerged for a time such as this to share my experiences and lessons learned. Although I spent many years suffering in silence, even when it seemed I had it all together; it will be worth it to know that a woman reading this book won't have to. Through God's grace, I'm still here, and there is still purpose to be fulfilled.

I once went to a phlebotomist who drew my blood with such care and precision that I never forgot him. If putting patients at ease during their doctor's visit is his purpose, why is this less important than former President Barak Obama's purpose to unify a nation, break stereotypes, and lead the free world as the first United States president of color. One of my girlfriends is hilarious. She brightens people's day with her humor and provides laughter as "good medicine."

Her kind of purpose can actually save a life or pull someone out of a dark place. We all know the housewife who quietly runs her household with the skill and tenacity of a CEO. The rooms she cleans, counseling she gives, and love demonstrated sometimes *is* her purpose.

Instead of us always expecting our God-ordained purpose to be a huge, monumental "thing" that will make us rich and famous, why not consider that there is a whole universe behind the scenes. Sometimes we are called to what appears to be thankless acts of service, yet in the eyes of God and the people impacted, they are huge. This is also purpose. Maybe you are an amazing helper or that friend who is always there for others.

My editor for this book also ghostwrites. Her name may never appear on a book cover, and she may never be famous for the many books she's helped produce, but she is clear that she is operating in her purpose in doing this work. God decides, not us. However, God intends to use you for the purpose for which He created you. You were put on this Earth to be a blessing to others through service. This *is* your purpose. And it's okay if it takes you some time to hear from Him or figure it out.

You Are Not Your Work

It's common in our society to meet someone and the next question is, "What do you do?" This has caused a tendency to self-identify based on our career or the type of work that we do. We know that one's purpose can be the same as what they do for a living, and careers like teaching and social work are sometimes chosen based on what you believe is your purpose. However, you are not your work, and your purpose usually has nothing to do with your vocation. This may be a hard pill to swallow for those who have attained a certain level of success in their careers and base their identities on this.

Some of you may remember Michael J. Fox, the five-time Emmy Awards, Grammy and Golden Globe Awards winning actor, well known for his role as Alex P. Keaton on the sitcom *Family Ties* in addition as his starring roles in *Spin City* and *Back to the Future,* among many more. I grew up watching him during his career which spans five decades. With all the awards and accolades, one would assume his purpose is sharing his undeniable talent with the world. However, his diagnosis of Parkinson's disease at just twenty-nine years old and the work he has done through his self-titled foundation is most likely his true calling. The world has watched on to see his public decline with the debilitating disease, but his purpose has been to inspire us all, as he's continued to work despite his physical limitations and with his wife of thirty-two years right by his side, as a demonstration of fortitude and real love.

Magic Johnson's claim to fame was being a professional athlete, but perhaps his purpose is more aligned with the many businesses he has successfully launched in underserved neigh- borhoods and the influence he has had on minority entrepreneurship.

In the 1990s movie, *The Pursuit of Happyness,*[23] Eric Gardner, played by Will Smith, was convinced that all his happiness and success hinged on being offered a position with a big financial brokerage firm. He figuratively went to hell and back, attempting to realize this dream, suffering through homelessness while being a single parent in pursuit of happiness. Yes, he ended up securing the position, and the ending credits let you know he started and sold his own firm years later, becoming a millionaire.

Despite the hopeful outcome and achieving his career goals, the movie was just as much about his special relationship with his son. Perhaps his real purpose was about breaking a generational cycle of poverty and struggle for his son and showing him and other young men by example what grit and determination can yield. The bottom line is, as you can see from some of these examples, that there is a price to pay to live your purpose, but you won't be fulfilled or content until you discover it and are walking in it for the glory of God.

We Are a Work in Progress

This may be hard to fathom, but I believe that your purpose may change from season to season. The Word of God tells us in the Amplified version of Ecclesiastes 3:1: "There is a season (a time appointed) for everything and a time for every delight *and* event *or* purpose under heaven." In different seasons, your purpose may be to focus on being a good mother, wife, caring for aging parents, a major life transition, or preparing for purpose. Every season may not be about actively pursuing or operating in the purpose God has unveiled, so seeking Holy Spirit guidance on the timing of being active in your purpose is critical.

A fruit out of season can kill you. You may remember the notorious fallout between Iyanla Vanzant and Oprah Winfrey over a decade ago. It appeared that Iyanla ended her business relationship with the Oprah Winfrey Show and Harpo Studios out of her frustration that Oprah had not, after twenty guest appearances, set her up with her own show as she had Dr. Phil or Nate Berkus.

The timing wasn't right for the studio, so Iyanla was asked to wait, and she agreed without hesitation. That is, until Barbara Walters of NBC and others started to dangle other offers of opportunity in front of her. Iyanla then allegedly went back to Harpo, according to reports, and said something like, *I know I said I would wait, but I have other offers now, so can we negotiate?* This didn't go over well with Harpo, and the rest is history. She went to the Barbara Walters platform but was expected to conform beyond her comfort level, so it did not work out. Fortunately, Iyanla and Oprah were able to come together a few years later and mend fences.

In hindsight, Iyanla agreed that she wasn't ready. Therefore, waiting as she had been advised would have yielded much better outcomes. The show which airs today, *Iyanla, Fix My Life,* was launched, and the rest is history. The moral of the story here is too much too soon can kill you, just like a fruit out of season. Like many of us, Iyanla was a work in progress. Maturing and refining was needed for her to reach the peak of her purpose potential. Patience and wisdom is required to wait this process out and seek God about His perfect timing for your purpose to fully unfold.

KEY MESSAGE: God Has a Plan for You!

Before you were formed in your mother's womb, God both knew you and ordained you for His purpose. You are here for no other reason than fulfillment of this purpose. There are no comparisons. It's between you and God only, and He decides, not you. You must believe He has a plan and purpose predetermined just for you. Prayer and guidance by the Holy Spirit is ultimately how you know beyond a shadow of a doubt that this "thing" is what you were designed to do. In the mean- time, there are a few questions you can ask yourself while soul searching and rid yourself of self-imposed barriers:

- What would I do for free if I could?
- What problem am I passionate about solving?
- What gifts or talents have I had as long as I can remember?
- What do I do naturally, without much stress or effort?
- What is the "thing" that I do that motivates me, makes me feel the most fulfilled and fills my heart with passion and joy?

I hope I haven't given the impression in this letter, dear sisters, that purpose is easy. It's not, but the meaning that it brings to your life is worth it. However, you must be willing to be inconvenienced by purpose, patient through the process, and sensitive to God's timing. This is what I know:

- There is purpose in your deliverance and your testimony.
- You are shaped and molded to the character and image of Christ when pursuing purpose.
- We cannot live beneath what we were created to be and be at peace.
- We are all purposed to love one another.
- There are no comparisons in purpose. You will never be successful trying to be someone else.
- God's timing is perfect.

We have no idea what others have to sacrifice to be who God made them to be, but their gifts have made room for them, as will yours. A purpose-filled life is your best life, so get ready, get ready, get ready. Your purpose is waiting.

SCRIPTURE TO LIVE BY:

Proverbs 19:21 (AMP)

"Many plans are in a man's mind, but it is the Lord's purpose for him that will stand (be carried out)" (Proverbs 19:21 AMP). This Word reminds us that nothing supersedes God's planned purpose for your life, not your will or your plans. It's okay to dream big, make plans, and develop strategy for your life. No one would disagree that these are good practices.

But we must be pliable in God's hand, like clay, willing to always submit to His will and the leading of the Holy Spirit concerning your life. Our Father designed your purpose and equipped you before you were even formed, so no one knows better than Him the perfect timing to ignite you, based on His complete plan. Stay connected to Him, so you can clearly hear and fulfill your purpose in His perfect season.

Letter 12:
DEAR WOMEN WHO ARE IN A GOOD PLACE

"I am the vine; you are the branches. If you remain in me and I in you, you will bear much fruit; apart from me you can do nothing, If you do not remain in me, you are like a branch that is thrown away and withers; such branches are picked up, thrown into the fire and burned. If you remain in me and my words remain in you, ask whatever you wish, and it will be done for you" (John 15:5-7 NIV).

You may have heard the saying, *I may not be where I want to be, but I am certainly not where I used to be.* Take a moment and reflect over something that has happened in your life that you did not think you were going to get through, or you thought you might lose your mind. One major event for me was when a relationship I was in did not go as I had expected, particularly since I just *knew* he was the one for me. My heart broke into pieces, and the type of pain I experienced was something I had never before experienced.

This is going to sound ridiculous, but it's the truth. I went to the drug store and asked the pharmacist was there any medication they had for a broken heart, since they had medication for everything else. The pharmacist told me they did not have anything, but he was pretty sure time would heal my heart. In retrospect, I know he laughed when I left, but nevertheless, I remained devastated during that time. That's a situation where I am happy to look back and say, "I may not be where I want to be, but I am not where I used to be."

Who in their right mind wants to endure trials, tribulations, hardships, or temptation that will test us or sometimes break us all the way down? Knowing there is no way to circumvent and we all will be impacted, I made a decision to let God be my anchor. In other words, instead of trying to figure out the why, it's time to accept that these experiences are inevitable. Sadly, some of them we may inflict on ourselves, like when we steal, smoke, drive while drinking or texting, participate in toxic platonic or romantic relationships, or being addicted to distractions like social media or other vices.

We all know there are consequences associated with everything we do. We live in uncertain times, and we cannot predict tomorrow. We can only hope and be grateful when God has blessed us to live another day. When He has graced us to do so, see it as a gift, a *present*.

Each day you are among the living, open your present and know that God has something special for you because you are special and have been uniquely, fearfully, and wonderfully made. You were created for a purpose, and this is why the NIV version of the book of James, chapter one, verses 2–17 relay a powerful narrative. The paraphrased version says, consider it joy when we go through trials and tribulations because perseverance will be produced, and we will become more developed and whole in our lives. If you lack anything, ask and believe according to what God has purposed for you, and you will receive.

Those of you who have persevered will be blessed because you were steadfast under trial, you will not be fearful for what you will suffer, and you will be faithful till death. Here's another example while I stay with the theme of relationships. I will spare the specifics of being in some not- so-good relationships over more than thirty years, but having a lifetime partner was always a strong desire of mine since graduating from college. Only God knows what I endured over this span of time.

Nevertheless, my mind was made up that maybe God's desire must be for me to be alone. I finally accepted it. Shortly thereafter, I ran into a high school friend in church that I had not seen in twenty-plus years. We spoke, but there was no attraction. About a year later, we ran into each other again, and I still had no interest. He then started pursuing me, and I prayed to God, "If this is the person you have for me, you will have to change my heart." He, too, was a man of God, and unbeknownst to me, his pursuit of me was done just how God knew I would like, and eventually my heart changed.

Two years later, we were married. One thing God revealed to me is if I had not experienced trials and tribulations with previous suitors, I would not have recognized a good man when I saw him. What a blessing it is to have a relationship with our Lord Jesus Christ. It's like a breath of fresh air to surrender your life to God, yes, a God you cannot see, but you can feel and experience in powerful ways. Actually, you *can* get to a place where you may see him. For example, I recall how spellbound I became when I witnessed the beauty of Maui, Hawaii. Man could not have created that beauty.

The process of committing to God will be worth it, but you will not be able to do it alone. There are people in your life who have been placed there for a reason or a season. I encourage you to have a personal board of directors, meaning individuals who serve as a source of advice and counsel with your best interest at heart. These are people with certain competencies or who may play a specific role in your life, such as financial planner, an attorney, mentor, spiritual advisor, friend who keeps it real, confidant, health, and wellness buddy, and others where you feel is appropriate for what you may need in your life at the time. You can gain strength from having great people around you, who will hold you accountable.

God has not always been my anchor; I was my own anchor. And many of you may be able to relate to that statement. For years I resisted and failed to embrace hardships and decided to suppress many of my feelings. I realized, after reading my journaling from over twenty-five years, that I suffered emotionally on the inside and sometimes presented as someone else outwardly. Ladies, these letters of love written to you on these pages have been in the making for over twelve plus years.

I did not want to be exposed and feared being authentic because I was more concerned about what people would think of me. So, rather than being obedient to what God had asked me to do, like write this book, I stayed in my own way. Self-imposed barriers have the propensity to keep you stuck and paralyzed from living your best life, the life God has intended for you to live. Have you felt, or are you feeling there is something else God has for you to do in addition to what you are doing now?

I am hopeful you will gain insight, tools, and resources that will empower you to step aside and allow God's purpose for your life to unfold. I am reminded of a quote by American professional baseball player, Jackie Robinson: "A life is not important except in the impact it has on other lives."[24] Imagine you being a blessing to many, and when you put yourself aside, you will see your life transform. These love letters to you signify that I've gotten me out of my way. I am declaring and decreeing in the name of Jesus that you, too, will break free and that the wisdom found in these pages will be a revelation and a renewed sense of empowerment and purpose for your life.

You will also trust God and be willing to go places that may be uncomfortable, but where you know you are being led as part of your God-ordained destiny. Don't take my word for it; take God's. Things will be so amazing when you have a mind-set to trust God to determine and guide everything about your life. Remember, faith without works is dead. We all have to do our part, and behaviors are based on our beliefs. As the saying goes, if you do not believe in anything, you will fall for everything.

This letter is addressed to women who may finally find yourself in a good place in life. Let's revisit what being in a good place means. Of course, it may have a different meaning for different people. One may be in a time in life where material things and status personifies a "good place," like a car, house, clothes, husband, partner, money, children doing well, ability to travel, and so forth. Career success, a certain position, or going back to school to pursue something different, may also signify your good place. Oh my goodness, what great things to attain, and once you have conquered several of these, what's next? You may find yourself with a lot of *things* and some extra time on your hands.

Take heed that an idle mind and too much time is a devil's workshop. This is a great time to keep moving and seek God about what else He may have in store for you. If you are still here and breathing, there is a "next" coming. I have been blessed with accolades and material things and *still* found it was not fulfilling, and even could be detrimental. We want people to love us for who we are, not for what we have.

My good place is peace of mind and contentment about what God is unfolding in my life today. I applaud you for being in your *good place*. Like me, resting in your good place still may not be your daily constant, but it will not be where you used to be either. By the grace of God, I am getting closer each day, and so will you.

KEY MESSAGE: Live Your Best Life

When the enemy fights you so hard, remember this is just a tactic to keep you from doing what God has for you to do. Life is not all about you, but invest in yourself and continue to learn, grow, and serve. Association brings about assimilation, so be careful who you hang out with. Having a relationship with God will feed your inner self. Every so often, ask yourself, "Am I living my best life?"

Remember the lesson of Jeremiah 29:11. Whatever you are experiencing now, just know God knows the plans He has for you, plans to prosper and give you a hope. Here's what I know.

- Don't give up because life is hard. Giving up is easy, but you are more than a conqueror,
- Know if God has given you His gift of the present, then He is not done with you yet.

- Do what you always wanted to do. Face your fears because that is the only way you will overcome them.
- Whatever you do, ask yourself, is it ethical, legal, and moral?
- Your latter days will be greater than your former. With God, it matters not how we start, but how we finish.
- Circumstances may not be different, but what you can change is how you look at things.
- Remember, people do not always remember what you said or done, but they will remember how you made them feel.

SCRIPTURE TO LIVE BY

Scripture: John 15:5-6 (KJV)

God has different ways of speaking to an individual, and one of the ways he speaks to me is through my dreams. In 1995, God revealed to me that without Him I can do nothing, and John 15:5-6 was the scripture that was shared during my process of dissecting the dream. It reads: "I am the vine, ye are the branches: He that abideth in me, and I in him, the same bringeth forth much fruit: for without me ye can do nothing. If a man abides not in me, he is cast forth as a branch, and is withered; and men gather them, and cast them into the fire, and they are burned."

My dream was full of branches and beautiful fruit, and the fruit kept falling out of the bag. and as soon as I gathered them to place them back in the bags, they rolled out again. That's the day I knew that if I remained in Him I would produce much fruit. Our Christian journey is a process. This is not about perfection; it is more about your progress.

Jesus is the true vine, and not only does the vine spread, but it is also deeply rooted, We are the branches. If we continue to abide in Him and He in us, we will bear much fruit in our lives. In Galatians 5:22–23 (NIV), the fruit will be love, joy, peace, patience, kindness, goodness, faithfulness, gentleness, and self-control. God knows those are attributes we need in this life. In the event we stop the connection with God, we will wither and will be picked up and cast in the fire.

My beautiful women who are in a good place, stay there. Stay connected to the vine, so you may witness your God, the source of your peace and purpose.

EPILOGUE

*"Behold, I will do a **new thing**; now it shall spring forth; shall ye not know it? I will even make a way in the wilderness, and rivers in the desert"*
(Isa. 43:19 KJV).

Self-imposed barriers, big or small, come in all shapes, sizes, and forms of manifestations. As you've walked with me through my back story and twelve plus year process to mitigate my self-imposed barriers, hopefully you have revisited scenes from your own journey. It should be evident that getting in your own way can show up in your life, wearing many hats and masks. It can manifest in many ways: insecurity, playing small, playing pretend, fear, procrastination, and mental or physical illness.

The good news, dear woman of God, is that God is fully in control, and He has a plan and purpose for your life—if you believe and choose to surrender to God. Through God's grace and mercy when you submit, there is redemption. Even your self-imposed delays, self-denials, and even your self-destruction can't thwart or undo what your Father in heaven has pre-ordained and destined for your life.

The Word of God tells us in Isaiah 43:19, "Behold, I will do a new thing; now it shall spring forth; shall ye not know it? I will even make a way in the wilderness, and rivers in the desert." This means this new chapter, new you, new life, will "appear" before you know it or are even aware that it's happening. So, don't give up and keep it moving. Not only will this new thing spring up, but it will show up for you even in the midst of a dry, deserted place, if you believe. In this place, He will create *in* you and *around* you, rivers of flowing water, which spring forth life.

Now, if that doesn't make you shout, what will? You have survived your own backstory, traumatic events meant to destroy you, and you thrived through COVID. So, now take a deep breath and submit. With your whole being, submit your will to His and pray for healing and divine direction. Watch God mitigate self-imposed barriers and strongholds to do a *new* thing in your life!

You will still face challenges, but God will give you confidence and boldness, as He directs and strengthens you through it all. Girl, move, and get out of your own way. It's time, and you are more than equipped *and* ready. What a blessing it is to find and be your true self.

If you were empowered by '*Is Your Way In Your Way?*' would you be so kind as to leave a review that will help others learn about the benefits of this book? Besides, your feedback helps improve the quality of my book.

Email: Mayo@CassandraCrawley.com

Website: www.CassandraCrawley.com

Thank you,

Cassandra Crawley Mayo

ENDNOTES

[1] *Author, Linda Ellis, Copyright 1996-2021 SW Inspire Kindness thedashpoem.com*

[2] Durabont, F. (Director). The Shawshank Redemption [Film]. Castle Rock Entertainment; Story by Stephen King, 1994.

[3] Holy Bible. New International Version, Zondervan Publishing House, 1984

[4] https://themindsjournal.com/dont-be-afraid-to-start-over

[5] Kim Parker, Pew Research Center, "Families may differ, but they share common values on parenting," Sept. 2014, www.pewresearch.org

[6] The Holy Bible, New King James Version copyright @1982 by Thomas Nelsons

[7] Dr. Phillip C. McGraw, *Self Matters: Creating Your Life from the Inside Out*, Simon & Schuster, Nov. 2001

[8] King, Martin Luther, Jr., 1929–1968. I Have a Dream; the Quotations of Martin Luther King, Jr., New York: Grosset, 1968.

[9] Juan Manuel "John" Quiñones (Host), What Would You Do? (American hidden camera TV program), American Broadcasting Company (ABC News Production), Feb. 2008.

[10] Theodore Roosevelt Collection. Houghton Library, Harvard University. Theodore Roosevelt Digital Library. Dickinson State University. Web. April 27, 2011. www.theodorerooseveltcenter.org

[11] Mohandas Karamchand Gandhi, www.wikipedia.com

[12] Read and Spell Blog, "Self Confidence vs. Self-Esteem," www.readandspell.com

[13] Joan Prodrazik, HuffPost.com, "Oprah On Forgiveness: This Definition Was 'Bigger Than An Aha Moment,'" Oprah Winfrey quote from Oprah's Lifeclass (OWN Network), March 11, 2013.

[14] Jaelline Jaffe, Jeanne Segal, and Lisa Flores Dumke, HelpGuide, "Emotional and Psychological Trauma: Causes, Symptoms, Effects, and Treatment," Sept. 16, 2005, www.helpguide.org

[15] Jennifer Robinson, *WebMD.com*, "The Effects of Stress on Your Body," Dec. 10, 2017

[16] *Forrest Gump* [film], Robert Zemeckis (director), Winston Groom (story by), The Tisch Company, July 6, 1994

[17] Mayo Clinic Staff, MayoClinic.org, "Chronic stress puts your health at risk," www.mayoclinic.org

[18] Robert Porter (medically reviewed by Lauren Fawley), BetterHelp.com, "Is Depression A Disease? Understanding The Facts," June 2, 2020, www.betterhelp.com.

[19] Pewtrusts.org, "The Case for Advance Care Planning," Aug. 19, 2015, www.pewtrusts.org.

[20] https://www.google.com/search?q=average+life+expectancy+in+the+US&ie=UTF-8&oe=UTF-8&hl=en-us&client=safari

[21] Leslie F. Church & Gerald W. Peterman (Editors), The NIV Matthew Henry Commentary, Zondervan, Jan. 1, 1992

[22] Nicole Johnson, Youtube.com, "The Invisible Woman" [Video], March 20, 2008, www.youtu.be/9YU0aNAHXP0

[23] *The Pursuit of Happyness* [Film], Gabriele Muccino (Director), Will Smith (Narrator), Columbia Pictures, Relativity Media, Overbrook Entertainment & Escape Artists, Dec. 15, 2006

[24] Jackie Robinson, www.jackierobinson.com (quotes).

Printed by Libri Plureos GmbH in Hamburg, Germany